# Bees and Spiders

# Bees
## and
# Spiders

Applied Cultural Awareness
and the
Art of Cross-Cultural Influence

Brian L. Steed

Strategic Book Publishing and Rights Co.

This book is based on an original article published in the
December 2009 issue of Army magazine that further developed
into a series of lectures presented in Iraq and the United Arab
Emirates from 2010–2013.

Strategic Book Publishing and Rights Co.
12620 FM 1960, Suite A4-507
Houston, TX 77065
www.sbpra.com

ISBN:978-1-62857-592-7

Book Design by Julius Kiskis

22 21 20 19 18 17 16 15 14    1 2 3 4 5

# Dedication

To the people of Jordan and the bedouin, who live a life of
devotion and have a perspective of generations.

To my great friend and companion,
the heart of my success, Sheri.

# Contents

# List of Figures

# Acknowledgments

As I stated in the dedication, I am most grateful for the people of Jordan. Specifically, I want to express my thanks to the officers and soldiers of the Electronic Reconnaissance Battalion, the Directorate of Military Intelligence, and all those with whom I interacted over my two and a half years of service and my five and a half years of involvement in that great country. They taught me, as much as it is possible for me to learn, what it means to be Arab and what it means to be Muslim. It was a true honor to learn from them. They treated me as a brother and friend. I still feel tremendous joy every time I meet or see any Jordanian in far-off places.

I want to express my gratitude to the people of Israel and the great and dedicated officers and soldiers of the Israeli Defense Forces. I am particularly grateful to those with whom I worked most closely in the Foreign Relations Branch of the Ground Forces Command. It was a joy and pleasure to experience the challenges and miracle that is modern-day Israel and the ancient and foundational beliefs that are Judaism.

I wish to express my profound gratitude for all the Arab and Muslim officers with whom I have worked from Iraq to Morocco, Turkey to Yemen. Each one provided another critical tessera in the mosaic of my understanding of the Arab–Muslim world.

I am grateful to Sam Hargrove and Rob Nye for allowing me the time and opportunity to develop the program of instruction and presentations that form the basis of this work. Their patience and support came in the midst of the complex and challenging world of Iraq and Operation New Dawn.

I am especially grateful to Michael Ferriter, who provided tremendous insights and patiently endured my comments, thoughts, and philosophizing. He is a truly great commander and one of the greatest leaders in the modern form of warfare.

I thank my family and friends, who have read and reviewed this book and consistently supported me throughout my professional and creative life.

# Preface

From 2005 to 2008, I regularly spoke to groups of US college students traveling in and through Jordan. During one such occasion a student asked me a question about the differences between Arab people and American people. In the mental struggle I went through in trying to determine how best to answer, I happened upon the analogy of bees and spiders. The intent was to express the depth and significance of the differences between the two cultures. These are not cosmetic differences, but fundamental and foundational, as if we were like *bees and spiders*, approaching the world from radically different perspectives. After using this metaphor on that occasion, I developed it over the course of several years and have presented it here.

The next step in the conceptual development of this simple statement into a more cogent argument was in the form of a paper to assist US military personnel who were preparing to or who were currently interacting with Arabs in Iraq and its neighboring countries. This paper was eventually published in December 2009 by *Army* magazine.

From 2008 to 2010, I used this metaphor to assist college students and military professionals during my service in Israel. In Israel I met several men who operated a company that offered cultural awareness training to both Israelis and foreigners, including US military. What made their approach unique and interesting was that they took their understanding of the Arabic language, Islam, and Palestinian culture and operationalized it. What this means is that they taught this information in a way that allowed the average person to apply and use it in their military operations or business interactions. This was critical in changing *bees and spiders* from an intellectual exercise into a practical approach that explains the differences in cultures and how to put that knowledge to use.

My service in Jordan and Israel put me in contact with US military officers who had served in Iraq. I was always disappointed when they described the cultural awareness training they had received prior to their deployments. Almost to a person their training focused on what I call Cultural Awareness 101: take things with your right hand, don't point the bottom of your feet at someone, don't stare at women, that sort of thing. After nearly seven years of fighting in Iraq (as of 2010), the US military had not matriculated to a graduate level of explaining the culture into which we were sending our soldiers. I was terribly frustrated by this failure.

In preparation for my own deployment to Iraq in the summer of 2010, I went through the standard cultural awareness training for an individual soldier and experienced this very problem. Though the training included mandatory online briefings that were quite informative, it involved no live interaction with people who had experience or expertise in the region. After arriving in Iraq I quickly noted that US personnel were frustrated by their interactions with Iraqi government and military leaders, and this interaction was doing little good—and sometimes great harm—to the US–Iraqi relationship. I really felt that the problem was people's limited understanding of Arab culture. There was disdain and distrust and little to no empathy.

Early in my service in Iraq a friend invited me to present a brief to his organization on regional issues, using my experience as a general topic. I decided to use the title from my earlier article: "Bees and Spiders: Seeing the World from Different Perspectives." The response was very positive and I was asked to come back and provide a presentation on how to apply the philosophy I had shared. These briefs evolved into a three-lecture series of four to five hours, which I have delivered more than a dozen times in Iraq and the United Arab Emirates. The limited possibility of travel in Iraq caused me to look at putting these lectures into book form.

Following my service in Iraq I was assigned to the United Arab Emirates, where I had direct interaction with US military and business professionals. It became clear that the challenges of cross-cultural engagement were not limited to US government employees. This is a much broader issue that includes governments, businesses, and people of all professions and interests.

I would further add that the principles and practices recommended here have great value in any cross-cultural environment and not simply those between Arabs and Americans.

# Introduction

D o not skip this. This is important to read.

> *In the Middle East there is no such thing as an expert—*
> *there are only varying degrees of ignorance.*
> —A roughly accurate quote from
> a Middle East Foreign Area Officer

Why should you listen to what I have to say in the pages to follow? I think this is a legitimate question and one that I hope everyone is asking at this point. Anyone who claims to be a Middle East expert is not someone you should listen to. That is because the Middle East is so vast in terms of cultures, history, religions, and various other issues that to be an *expert* for this entire region is just not possible.

I am not an expert.

*Then why should I read this?* one should be asking.

The simple answer is that what is presented in the following pages is a unique and useful perspective of how to understand Arabs and the Middle East that is derived from years of experience working with the average man and woman on the street.

I do not intend to write a biography or present my accomplishments, but simply to explain why the perspective used in this book is worth listening to.

I have studied the Middle East for more than twenty years.

So what? one should exclaim. There are many who have studied the Middle East, and that should not be sufficient cause to buy and read a book from them. In addition to regional study, I have also spent a great deal of time being, thinking, and fighting like an opponent—thinking *like the other,* if you will. My experience serving in the Opposing Force of the US Army National Training Center and researching the behavior of opponents of the US military was critical to developing the method of explanation in this book.

If that is not enough for the reader, then I hope the following regional experience will suffice.

I served continually in the Middle East from January 2005 until June 2013. Time in the region is not enough. I have met many people who have lived in the Middle East years longer than I have. The difference is that the majority of my service was in a culturally immersed environment. For example, I served as a battalion deputy commander and staff officer in the Jordanian army for two and a half years. Immediately following that I served as a liaison to the Israel Defense Forces with my office on an Israeli military base. I have traveled from Morocco to Iraq and from Turkey to Yemen meeting and speaking with common working people in sixteen different countries in the region. I have also served in US and NATO organizations in Iraq and the United Arab Emirates.

The type and location of service matter. Each day I worked with and spoke to regular Jordanians, Israelis, and people of other nationalities and ethnicities throughout the region. I saw the wisdom and ignorance present at the street level. I also sat in conferences and symposia with some of the most educated scholars from both Western and Middle Eastern countries. There is a profound difference in understanding and outlook between the educated elite and the basic working man and woman.

This provided me with an understanding of how average people in these countries think. I think this provides a unique perspective worthy of note.

I have seen the challenges and frustrations faced by Americans and Europeans as they interact with their Arab counterparts. I am familiar with the failure to properly prepare Westerners to work in the Middle East and the damage this does to cross-cultural relationships.

I have also seen that the Arab world is not simply the Levantine world.[1] Nor is it the Egyptian, Arabian Peninsula, or Mesopotamian worlds. Describing the Arab people in a single brushstroke is as dangerous as describing Americans in a single brushstroke. I know that because I have seen and personally experienced it.

I believe that these combined experiences of academic research and study, applied military operations as *the other*, and time spent working and living with the people in the region give me a unique and beneficial perspective for writing a book designed to help Westerners function and succeed in the Arab world. I hope you will agree.

---

[1] The Levant is the Eastern Mediterranean and is typically considered to consist of Syria, Lebanon, Israel, and Jordan.

# Why Does This Matter?

*All US forces are to withdraw from all Iraqi territory,
water, and airspace no later than the 31st of December
of 20112*

—US–Iraq Status of Forces Agreement

When I was getting ready to deploy to Iraq in the summer of 2010 and I spoke with people in the US, they often commented, "I thought we were out of Iraq." In late September of 2010, I was sitting in the dining facility at Forward Operating Base Union III in Baghdad, Iraq, as I watched a reporter riding in a STRYKER armored vehicle declare that he was riding with the last combat troops leaving Iraq. I looked around at the uniformed service members sitting with me, who all carried a weapon and wore body armor every day, to ask, "What are we, then?"

I know that we ended the operations leaving Iraq and many may think that a book about cross-cultural interactions between Arabs and Americans may be superfluous. But with possible US involvement in the Syrian civil war and a general misunderstanding of the events associated with the Arab Spring, there is an existing and continuing need.

While I hope that the US will not again deploy tens of thousands of military forces to the Middle East, I strongly believe that this

---

[2] Unofficial translation of the US–Iraq Status of Forces Agreement signed by both parties in November 2008. The specific quote was taken from the website http://www.mcclatchydc.com/2008/11/18/56116/unofficial-translation-of-us-iraq.html.an.

book has relevance for several important reasons.

1. This book is not just for the military. Business, government, and religious leaders who interact with the Middle East will also benefit from it. I have seen that similar frustrations exist in any cross-cultural exchange, and I believe that the lessons and discussion here will benefit all such relationships.

2. This book challenges the assumptions that Americans and US military personnel make about ourselves that impede our ability to develop empathy with another culture.

3. The Middle East remains a critical region in strategic and economic terms. Americans need to better understand how to interact and function here.

4. The lessons in this book apply to any cross-cultural relationship in general and to relationships with tribal-based cultures specifically.

# Warnings and Disclaimers

**D**o not treat this like the warnings on so many of your household appliances. Read this. It will help put what follows in a more reasonable context.

When I teach this topic as a series of classes, I begin each one with a warning or disclaimer. I believe it is important to do the same here. This is done to help the reader understand what is not intended or being said and thereby be better prepared to understand the material presented.

### Warning One

Any book written with the intent of describing a large group of people runs a great risk of creating a stereotype that can lead to prejudice and racism. It is also true that a book seeking to explain or describe 300 million people in simplistic terms will just be plain wrong.

The intent is not to create such negative feelings. Quite the contrary. I have found that the more I teach this subject, the more I appreciate and respect the Arab people and Arab culture.

### Warning Two

The analogy is simple and therefore has flaws. It is inaccurate to describe a people from so many different countries and regions who speak so many very different dialects as one type of people.

Think of how you might explain Americans (assuming you are an American) to someone from a different country. Three hundred million people living across three thousand miles from east to west just are not the same people—there are a variety of subcultures and groups with unique differences in behavior, dialect, and culture.

The Arab world has about the same number of people and is spread over a geographic area of about the same size. Arabs have the additional challenge of having separate nationalities, which adds to their differences.

Where differences exist that I have seen and experienced, those will be stated to provide a fuller and more complete picture of the analogy.

That said, one can look at the United States and make some broadly accurate statements about Americans, and these broad statements have a value in their accuracy of helping people to better understand Americans.

It is this type of perspective that I am working toward—broadly accurate statements to assist in shaping and framing thinking.

### Warning Three

Any analogy can be taken too far. People are not *bees or spiders*. The use of such a metaphor or analogy is to create a mental image useful in shaping how one prepares for and thinks about one's engagements. I can imagine some zoologist or anthropologist reading this and thinking, "That is not how a bee really behaves," or as one person expressed to me, "You ascribe individual behavior to a collective creature." Please do not extend the meaning beyond what is reasonable or useful. I do not.

### Warning Four

This book begins with philosophy of difference and a way of

thinking about cross-cultural relationships. It is not a list of do's and don'ts, though there are some of those throughout the book. This is about how to think about the interaction.

### Warning Five

There will be redundancies in examples and explanations. These are intentional overlaps, as not all examples apply equally—some are narrow and others broad. One may prove more useful in a given context than another, and therefore the more examples provided the better, even if they are more or less redundant.

### Final Warning

This is not a comprehensive book on cultural awareness or a sociological or anthropological dissertation on the Arab people and culture. This is not a discourse on Islam or a comprehensive geographic explanation of the Middle East, the Arab world, or the Islamic world.

This is a method or a way to think about cross-cultural relationships. This should help one recognize perspectives and to perceive motivations—one's own and those of one's counterpart. I hope, most sincerely, that this will provide a viable method to develop empathy—the how of that most challenging of inter-human skills.

### Disclaimer One

Most of the names of individuals and their countries have been changed or removed. I have done this not to avoid accuracy, but to avoid recriminations or unintended embarrassment. The point is not to belittle a country or its people. The stories in this book have been included to illustrate points, not to make fun or be insulting or degrading. In some cases the stories may create a sense of shame or the loss of honor, and this is something that I expressly want to avoid.

### Disclaimer Two

This book is not a recipe. One cannot simply add a cup of understanding and a tablespoon of empathy and two pinches of Arabic phrases and then have a gourmet relationship. Cross-cultural communication and relationship building is an art. I believe that it is one of the most challenging things human beings do. Each reader will need to pick and choose from the lessons in this book and adapt them to their specific circumstances and the personalities of those they interact with.

I certainly believe that if one adopts the philosophy outlined here, one will have greater success in future interactions and relationship building.

### Apology

Lest I offend any of my Arab or Israeli friends who read this, or any other Arab or Israeli for that matter, I'd like to explain my purpose. My intent is to help those with less experience recognize some aspects of your culture so that they can better function within it. It is not my intent to belittle or insult you or your culture. As I have stated in my dedication, I love and respect the Middle East and the cultures and peoples found there. I sincerely hope that this book will assist in the communication of peoples.

If any who read this are offended, then I sincerely apologize and ask for your forgiveness.

# What Is an Arab?

I believe that what is contained in this book has value beyond a US–Arab context. Part of that value is the application of the principles and issues discussed to different cultures. In such a light, it is important to briefly discuss one of the cultures in question.

What is an Arab? I have asked this question in a variety of settings and I get a variety of answers. Some of those answers follow.

- One who speaks Arabic
- One who lives in the Middle East
- One from the Arabian Peninsula
- One who is Muslim
- One who has a common "Arab" culture

There are other answers as well, but these capture the difficulty in answering this question. As one thinks about what makes a person of a particular group, a lot of preconceived notions and prejudices can arise. In each of these five answers are exceptions and significant issues. Depending on one's experience in the Middle East, one may or may not see these flaws.

There is no simple answer to this question. For example, one day's Arab is another day's Egyptian. I will address some of the challenges with each of the above answers and then give the broad definition used in this book.

### *One who speaks Arabic*

Many people speak Arabic. Depending on the census and statistics, the number exceeds 300 million people. These people have a variety of religions and ethnicities, and many would take offense at being called Arabs, as they have their own distinct cultural identities.

For example, Arabic speakers include Kurds, Berbers, Jews, Copts, Turkomen, and Persians. Each of these groups would say they are not Arab. There are others as well. The Middle East is rich with thousands of years of history, and numerous peoples have moved into and through it, adapting culture and shared language and behavior. The common language does have an impact in creating a shared identity, but it is dangerous to think that all who speak the same language have the same identity. That would be similar to calling all who speak the English language Englishmen or Englishwomen.

### *One who lives in the Middle East*

Same challenge as above and even more. Persians, Turks, and numerous smaller groups have lived in the Middle East for centuries but are not Arab. Add to that the millions of expatriates who have moved to the region over the past half century or more to live and work. Location alone does not identify people as a common group.

### *One from the Arabian Peninsula*

This is probably the most definite yes, in that those who come from this part of the world are Arab. This is also the narrowest definition. Even though it is accurate to say that people from the Arabian Peninsula are Arabs, it is also important to note that Yemen (on the southwestern corner of the Arabian Peninsula) had a large Jewish population for centuries. There are many

Yemeni Jews living in Israel today. Are they Arab? Normally, the answer would be no, although I have met a handful who answer that question with a definite yes. Once again there is the exception of the expatriate residents who live and work on the Arabian Peninsula and have for decades and generations. They are typically not Arab.

### *One who is a Muslim*

From the narrowest definition of Arab to the broadest. As the broadest definition, this is the least accurate. Muslims include more than a billion people from Indonesia and the Philippines to Morocco and the United States and Canada. Of this number about 300 million or so speak Arabic. The countries with the three largest Muslim populations are Indonesia, Pakistan, and India. The Muslims of none of those countries consider themselves Arab.

Islam is a rich and diverse religion. It is true that Islam began in the Arabian Peninsula and that much of modern Arab culture is infused with Islamic culture and vice versa. In the modern Middle East it is so difficult to separate Islamic and Arabic cultures that one can describe it as having a combined Islamic–Arabic culture. The size and diversity of modern Islam makes this definition the most problematic.

### *One who has a common "Arabic" culture*

The definition of common culture is vague, and therefore this is probably the most accurate answer. In this sense of culture I use a broad definition, including language, behaviors, and self-identity. In essence, Arabs are those people who speak like Arabs, act like Arabs, and think they are Arabs. This includes many people in the Middle East and North Africa. It includes Muslims and Christians. It includes people who will say in some circumstances that they are Arab but in other times and places identify themselves more with their nation or religion. For the most part, this book will apply this definition when using the word "Arab."

I appreciate that this brief discussion has not been extremely definitive. I do hope that it has caused the reader to consider what one means when attaching the label "Arab" to a person. I further hope that this has also caused the reader to reflect on the diversity, dynamism, and depth of the modern Middle East.

# Part ONE
## Philosophy

# Philosophy

*Boxes, boxes, everywhere, and not any room to think.*[3]

—Paraphrase

The phrase think *outside the box* is a common one. The challenge that I want to discuss here is that there is not a singlebox that we need to think out of.[4]

The boxes discussed in this context are layered. This could be a long and deep sociological discussion, but for the sake of the ideas presented in this book I will be brief. Our layers of boxes include those created by society, culture, and personal experience. So when we think outside the box, which box are we thinking outside of?

I have regularly heard senior leaders in the military congratulate a subordinate for thinking *outside the box,* but upon reflection the subordinate was simply thinking outside one box represented by that specific commander's perspectiveand understanding rather than truly being innovative.[5] This very

---

[3] Paraphrase from *The Rime of the Ancient Mariner* by Samuel Taylor Coleridge. The original line is "Water, water, everywhere, And all the boards did shrink; Water, water, everywhere, Nor any drop to drink."

[4] This topic was addressed in some depth in my book *Piercing the Fog of War: Recognizing Change on the Battlefield: Lessons from Military History, 216 BC Through Today,* published in 2009 by Zenith Press. For ease of reference I will simply refer to it as Piercing the Fog of War from here on.

[5] It could more accurately be stated as "that is thinking outside my box."

narrow definition of *the box* is arguably the most common understanding of this phrase.

John Boyd, a military theorist and truly innovative thinker, posited that to *think outside the box* one must first destroy one's own box, that destruction of the old construct is necessary to precede the creation of a new construct.[6] As I came to understand Boyd's thinking I started to realize that it takes a genuinely exceptional mind to accomplish this, and therefore it would be nearly impossible for an average person to achieve. In *Piercing the Fog of War* I explained a way for a normal person to accomplish something similar, but without the need for a complete destruction of one's initial worldview. Here I will present a specific application of that same process with respect to gaining empathy of a different culture for the purpose of achieving a measure of influence.

In the accompanying figures I illustrate two opposing individuals in their respective conceptual boxes. For ease of explanation, they are in a single box rather than the layered boxes previously expressed. Rather than destroying an individual's box, it may be possible to expand that box in such a way that it can encompass the box of the counterpart or opponent. Once this is achieved, it is possible to see the possibilities and limitations perceived by the counterpart or opponent.

---

[6] This is explained in his paper Destruction and Creation which has been available on various internet sites.

# Growing the Box

**Counterpart /
Opponent**   **Us**

Us and Our Counterpart/Opponent

**Counterpart /
Opponent**   **Us**

Seeing the World from Separate Boxes

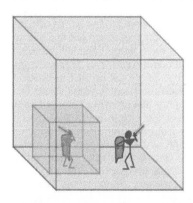

Seeing the World from a Box that Includes the
Counterpart/Opponent's Box

How do we grow our box? This is at the heart of what this book will try to explain. In *Piercing the Fog of War* I provide nine strategies to address how to prepare for and function withinan event of aberrational change.[7] I want to use three of

---

[7] The nine strategies discussed are: 1) Introspection (A strategy of self-reflection. The ability to see oneself and one's abilities, skills, resources, and attributes in an honest and full manner.); 2) Empathetic Appreciation (This strategy addresses the important aspect of having empathy for the opponent. To see the opponent as he or she sees himself or herself.); 3) Empathetic Expectation (The difference from the preceding strategy lies in the ability to recognize the possibilities imagined by the opponent. What does the opponent expect? Subsequently, how will the opponent react to the actions that one plans to conduct?); 4) Study of Language (So many issues, problems, and conflicts have begun and continue because of the confusion of language. Language is how humans translate thoughts into communicable directions and intent. Language needs to be understood as the opponent understands it.); 5) Study of History (This is a principle of precedent. What are the precedents in this region, on this subject, in this field? How did these precedents develop in the past? The Spanish-American philosopher and poet George Santayana's great statement about those not understanding history—"Those who do not remember the past are condemned to repeat it" (The Life of Reason, Volume 1, 1905)—is at the heart of this strategy.); 6) Study of Culture (Language and culture are two pillars of achieving empathy. Whereas empathetic appreciation and expectation are specific to an opponent, culture deals more broadly with the society from which that opponent comes.); 7) Multiple Reserves (Mid- and high-level leaders can only influence events in the heat of conflict by the allocation of resources; therefore, it is critical in times of potential aberration that leaders avoid limiting themselves to a single reserve that can only be committed at a single moment.); 8) Initiative (The participant who has the initiative and who directs the events can often determine who suffers from an aberration. The intent of this strategy is to get ahead of the decision cycle of the opponent and make him or her react to one's own decisions and actions rather than the alternative. It can also be described with the word preemption, the displacement of the opponent in time or space. This strategy removes the opponent from a position of advantage before he or she acts.); 9) Think Science Fiction (As a strategy of creativity, this requires a mind open to possibilities that may, on the surface, appear to be completely unconnected with the events at hand. This is the ability to reach out and draw from a variety of sources. This includes the use of creative minds that have considered the future and proposed seemingly fanciful or far-fetched solutions or realities.)

these strategies here.

### *Introspection*

The first strategy is *introspection*. This is to look inside to understand oneself, one's culture, and more specifically one's organization. This strategy is first for a reason. This is where cross-cultural empathy hits its first snag. Not taking the time to understand why one thinks the way one does makes it extremely difficult to understand another person's perspective. I will present this in a graphic way later, but for now it is essential to take the time to reflect on why one holds on to their beliefs and ideas. Are one's standards truly standard?

An example comes from a discussion with US pilots who worked with an Arab air force. They expressed the challenges of communicating US safety practices and standards, particularly the importance of crew rest before the duty day. The Arab pilots did not understand or accept this for some time. I reflected with the pilots on the history of the US Air Force regarding strategic airlift (cargo aircraft) and strategic bombing, which began in large measure in World War II to supply allied forces on multiple continents and to bomb distant targets. US pilots learned the importance of resting before a flight because they flew long hours over thousands of miles. Developing standards for crew rest was essential for the long-term survival of pilots and aircraft. Following World War II, strategic bombing became even more critical, as well as the ability to reinforce and resupply Europe. This meant establishing standards for crews being able to fly ten-thousand-plus miles.

Very few militaries outside the US have the need to fly such extreme distances. Arab air forces are no different, and thus they did not develop similar standards.

This example shows the benefits that come from introspective thinking. Once this historical perspective was understood, then it was possible for the US pilots to move beyond the prejudicial thinking that Arab pilots are not as good or poorly trained, and perceive their own view to be based on the culture and history of their own set of boxes.

Without this understanding it is very difficult to successfully move forward and start to understand another culture. One must first define clearly and completely one's own box before the box of the counterpart or opponent can be understood to any real measure of effectiveness.

### Empathetic Appreciation

The second strategy is *empathetic appreciation.* This refers to understanding the other person, culture, or organization. Why are they the way they are? Understanding is a prerequisite for empathy, as will be discussed in some detail in Part Two of this book. This is seeing the other through their eyes, so to speak.

### Empathetic Expectation

The third strategy is *empathetic expectation.* How will the other person, culture, or organization react, respond, or behave in a given situation? Seeing the world from someone else's eyes is not the same as seeing their expectation and possibilities. Just because one can see what the other person sees does not mean one can understand their interpretation of what they are seeing. Once one can see the world and the possibilities in it from a counterpart or opponent's perspective, it actually becomes possible to influence that person, culture, or organization. But not before.

# The Pyramid

Pyramid

From the Top

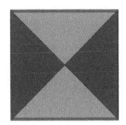

From the Side

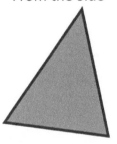

From the Bottom

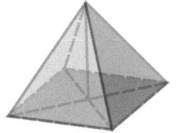

The Pyramid in its Complex
Three-Dimensional Shape

### *The Pyramid*[8]

A visual analogy of this comes through a reference to the geometric pyramid shape. Think of it in three dimensions, as the accompanying illustrations convey. When this shape is seen from different angles, it is perceived in radically different ways. If one looks at a pyramid precisely from the top, then one sees a square with bisecting diagonals. If one looks at the pyramid from the exact opposite direction, then one sees only a square. If one looks at the pyramid from the side, then one sees only a triangle. And if one looks at it from another angle, then one may see it in its complex three-dimensional shape.

*Introspection* is understanding the angle from which you are observing the pyramid. What do I see? Why does it look this way to me? These are fundamental questions for moving forward. *Empathetic appreciation* is recognizing the angle from which your counterpart or opponent is observing the pyramid. What does he or she see? Why does it look that way to him or her? Once these two conceptual understandings exist, then—and I would argue only then—one can effectively begin to anticipate how one's counterpart or opponent will respond to the events surrounding both the participants in the negotiation, conflict, or engagement.

---

[8] This analogy is used in Piercing the Fog of War as well. This is a specific application of that general analogy.

# We Are Different

*Vive la difference.*[9]

—French saying

I have four children. I went through the full measure of children's educational television, and I am myself a product of the early *Sesame Street* generation. I recall well many of the songs and phrases made famous by *Sesame Street.* There is one song in particular that I want to point out—"I've Got Two Eyes." In this song the emphasis is on the fact that because human beings have the same features, we are generally the same inside as well. Multicultural education in the US served and still serves a critical and necessary purpose: helping people from widely different backgrounds, cultures, ethnicities, and native languages to live and work together. In this vein this education style has succeeded.

In preparing Americans to function in a cross-cultural engagement, it has done a great disservice.

A personal experience comes from 2005, when I worked in the US embassy annex in Baghdad—Saddam Hussein's presidential palace. I worked with a variety of organizations to develop a plan to effectively engage the tribes of Iraq. In the process of discussions with a counterpart in the Department of State, we both shared how we taught cultural awareness. This

---

[9] This phrase literally means "life to the difference" but roughly translates as "celebrate the difference."

lady explained that she spent a great deal of time expressing the similarities of the two cultures. I shared that I spent a great deal of time on the differences. This concerned her, as she found that the more people see differences, the more they judge the other culture as inferior. I shared that my emphasis on difference was so that people would be better prepared for differences in understanding rather than assume agreement.

My opinions have not changed. Rather, the longer I have served in the region, the more I have seen that people make more errors by assuming agreement or common understanding than they gain through the goodwill of seeing similarities and value in the other culture.

I think it very dangerous for cultural arrogance to exist and perpetuate throughout a relationship. There are definitely things that one culture may do better than another, but across the broad spectrum it is dangerous to assume superiority based on the fact that *the other* is not like me.

There is no doubt that human beings across cultures and regions share a great deal. The differences between us are nuanced and small. Maybe the vast majority of things are shared based on our genes or a common ancestor. That said, I would like to reflect on the fact that our closest nonhuman genetic relative is the chimpanzee, which shares more than 98 percent of our genetic material. That means the difference between Leonardo da Vinci, with his brilliant intellect and creative genius, and a mud- and feces-throwing chimpanzee is less than 2 percent.

The point of this comparison is to say that the nuances that I previously acknowledged are VERY important. The nuances matter!

We are different. The difference is not in our number of eyes, ears, toes, or hair follicles, but in how we think and perceive the world—the way we perceive the pyramid.

As an exchange officer in the Jordanian Army, I sat in several key meetings with my Jordanian superiors and representatives of the US government. Typically these meetings were conducted in English. The Jordanian officers present had a great command of the English language. In many cases, after the meetings ended I would spend anywhere from fifteen to forty-five minutes explaining what was intended. The words were understood but the meaning was not clear, as both parties perceived the same words to have different meanings. What happened was that the Americans assumed the Jordanians understood what was being said because they spoke English so well. But though the basic meaning was clear, the underlying goals and desires were not and required a lot of post-meeting explanation.

This has proven to be true regardless of the country in which I have served.

From 2008–2010, I served in Israel and hosted delegations that met with the Israel Defense Forces (IDF) to discuss training and doctrine issues. A common topic of discussion in these meetings was the benefit of noncommissioned officers, who are known as NCOs in the US lexicon and sergeants in the IDF. The US officers and NCOs also use the term sergeant, and as both sides talked about sergeants and their importance to the unit, neither side understood that they were not talking about the same thing. An IDF sergeant has two to three years of experience in service, and that is all. A US NCO has four to twenty-six years of experience and years of cumulative professional schooling at the higher ranks. Neither side was talking about the same thing, but used the same word and were content in their belief that a sergeant is a sergeant.

The ability to recognize differences empowers a negotiator or a counterpart to better explain and discuss the primary issues at hand without preconceived notions of universal vocabulary or some elusive common sense or understanding. It forces one to be explicit rather than being tempted by the implicit.

The progression from ignorance of a foreign culture to empathy can be described in the three stages and attendant exclamations below. This is the path of progression this book tries to lead down.

Information       "How odd!"
Understanding    "I get it!"
Empathy          "I see!"

Even though we all have two eyes, we do not see the world the same. This is one of the most important points of this book, and is necessary to accept to make the recommendations that follow effective. If you do not believe it now, there are more examples to come.

Differences are not a bad thing. In the spirit of the opening quote for this section, we should *celebrate the difference.*

# Thought Questions

As I returned home each day from work at the Jordanian battalion, my wife would ask me, "What did you do today?" Each day I would answer, "Nothing." I was frustrated and felt like I wasn't accomplishing anything of value. This lasted for several weeks and months until I became exasperated with my answer, so I asked my wife to stop asking me.

My days in the battalion included an hour or more in the battalion commander's office, where we sat and drank coffee and tea[10] while various officers and soldiers came in and shared drinks, pleasantries, or received disciplinary actions. I felt like I was just sitting there and wasting my time, hence the frustration.

My thought questions are these:

1. Why are you here? (*Here* may be whatever cross-cultural environment you are in.)

Are you here to accomplish tasks?

Or are you here to create an environment of influence?

2. Is sitting in a person's office drinking coffee and tea for an hour and a half a waste of time?

I hope that by the end of this book readers will develop their own answers to these questions. I will provide my thoughts on them at the end.

---

[10] I actually drank an herbal bedouin drink, as religious practices kept me from drinking coffee and tea.

# Bees

---

This is a bee-centric description. The comparison comes later.

As I explain what a bee is with respect to this book, I ask for a measure of imagination. There will be elements of the bee as I describe it that come from nature itself, as well as elements that will seem to have come from an animated movie.

Imagine what a bee thinks about and what motivates it as it goes forth from its home out into the world. How does that bee measure success, and how might it describe its day to its spouse when it returns home? I know that bees do not really go to work and come home to talk with their spouse about their day, so use the sense of imagination I referenced above.

The bee in question sees its day and its success in terms of things it has to do. As it flies away from home the bee is thinking, *I have to collect pollen from four hundred flowers today. The field where the flowers are located is about two hundred meters from the hive. It will take me about thirty seconds to fly each way, and I can collect pollen from ten flowers with each trip. That means that I need to make forty trips, with each trip taking at least fifteen minutes. That is a ten-hour workday.*

As the bee flies to the field, he sees another field of flowers that have just blossomed and that represent a more desirable source of nectar. The bee will turn around and return to the hive, where it will conduct a dance that effectively communicates the location, direction, distance, and type of flowers in the find. The vibrating dance will communicate this information quickly and efficiently so that the group can react to the new information and redirect resources to take advantage of the opportunity.

In this image of the internal workings and external behavior of the bee, we already see the key elements of the analogy I want to make.

First, the bee is task oriented. It is a creature of to-do lists or agenda items. Success in many ways is defined in this concept of doing.

Second, the bee is analysis driven. The bee thinks about how far to fly, how long it will take, how many flowers are in the field, how many trips are required. In most ways this analysis is conscious and explicit.

Third, the bee believes in information sharing. It is best to share information with the greatest number of members of the community in the fastest way possible. Survival can be seen as based on information sharing.

Fourth, the bee has a god's-eye or map perspective of the world. The bee sees the world from above and therefore can perceive order where at the ground level there may only be chaos.

In summary, a bee is task oriented, analysis driven, information sharing, and has a map perspective.

# Spiders

This is a spider-centric description. The comparison comes later.

As with the bee, I ask for a measure of imagination with regard to my description of the spider. There will be elements of the spider as I describe it that come from nature itself, as well as elements that will seem to have come from an animated movie. Please continue the journey with me.

If the spider was to lie on a therapist's couch and the therapist were to say, "Tell me how you see yourself," I believe the spider would have a split self-definition. It would see itself in terms of itself as a spider, a living creature, but would also define itself in terms of its web. What is important about the web is everything: its strength, location, size, and effectiveness in capturing food or bringing resources to the spider. In this case the web is connected not simply to twigs and branches, but also to other spiders or the webs of the other spiders. This dually defined nature is important in understanding the spider's motivations and thinking.

The spider spends all day, every day, making and strengthening web connections. If there is a to-do list for the spider, this is it. I believe that a spider would not see this as a task, but rather as just what a spider does. Initial meetings and discussions are designed to establish a connection, and then later meetings and time together further add to and strengthen the connection.

The spider does not conduct analysis; the analysis is socially intuitive. The spider wants to be connected to those other spiders that will provide the greatest opportunity for gaining resources. Everyone just gets it; they all understand who the providers are. Analysis is unconscious and implicit.

Imagine a spider that has a web along a great trail in the woods. On this trail fly hundreds of bugs every day, and the spider's web is ideally positioned to catch most of them. What would happen if that spider were to go out and tell all his spider buddies the location of his web and how great the spot is? Other spiders would build their webs in the same area. What would then happen to our spider? His daily collection of food would dwindle significantly—he would have fewer resources. His very life may even be placed at risk by sharing this information. This is a very important point. **To a spider, sharing information is potentially self-destructive and potentially life threatening.** In this understanding, information is about resources—gaining them and providing them.

The ideal of a spider is to have a great web connected to many other powerful spiders with strong cords, so that it can simply sit back in the middle of his web, pull on a cord, and cause other spiders to respond to his wishes and will.

Finally, a spider's perspective of the world is a street-level perspective. Imagine sitting in that web as bugs come flying at you all day. It is not unlike sitting on a street and watching the cars approach. This is down in the weeds, maybe even literally. The world looks chaotic and a little crazy from this perspective.

In summary, the spider is dually defined (self and web), conducts implicit analysis, hoards information, builds his web, and has a street-level perspective.

# Comparison

This comparison is a cursory look at the bees and spiders analogy as applied to the specific cross-cultural relationship between Americans and Arabs. It is extremely useful to keep in mind that there are Americans who are spiders in their behavior and Arabs who are bees. It is in the military and the business community where the differences are the most apparent. Based on my experience I use the two militaries as the point of comparison.

### Focus
### *Americans: Task Focused*

Americans are task focused. The very existence of so many products designed to help manage to-do lists stands as a great example of this. Certainly military personnel are driven to accomplish things.

### *Arabs: Relationship Focused*

Arabs are all about relationships. They call each other just to say hello and maintain a connection. They have simple meetings that appear to an outsider to accomplish very little, but the point is to cast out that silk strand in the intent of strengthening the relationship. The nature of their relationships is how they define themselves. If they cannot be directly connected to the primary resource provider (president, king, sheikh, et cetera), then they want to be connected to the king's brother. If not that, then the king's cousin, so that they can draw a connection in as few stages as possible.

### *Loyalty*

Americans: Duty, Honor, Country, Bureaucratic Loyalty

The US military system of loyalty is driven by an ethic that emphasizes the code taught at the US Military Academy at West Point: Duty, Honor, Country. We serve out of a sense of what we should do, what we should be, and service to our country. These conceptual ideas are linked to a bureaucratic assignment system that places officers and soldiers in units with others with whom they have no prior relationship and expects unwavering obedience and loyalty. Our service is expected to be exemplary because of these ideas. We support and obey based on the assignments and these expectations.

When I served in Iraq from 2010–2011, I worked for two different bosses in two different jobs. In both cases I had never met the man before. I had no connection with either prior to our association, and it was possible that I might not see either of them again. The US military expected that I maintain a fierce loyalty to each during the time I worked for him, and that when I changed from one boss to another, the loyalty should immediately switch to the new.

If one seriously considers this way of thinking it seems slightly absurd. The only reason that person A or person B receives my loyalty is because I have been bureaucratically assigned to work for them. No other reason. This is what I mean when I talk about bureaucratic loyalty.

### *Arabs: Hospitality, Honor, Family (Tribe) Loyalty*

I was conducting a reconnaissance of the Jordanian border with another Jordanian Army officer and two soldiers. We met an officer of the Jordanian Badia police, bedouins with the responsibility of maintaining the security of that portion of the border. He was to accompany us throughout our initial reconnaissance, a trip that was to last three days. This officer was in his Class B uniform (a button-up shirt and dress pants) rather than a field uniform, as he thought he was supposed to go home for several days' leave. The Jordanian officer traveling with me chastised the Badia officer for not being properly clothed. We explained our plan, which included staying at a Badia police station that first night. We departed a short while later with our three vehicles: two army and one Badia. Throughout the course of the day the Badia vehicle seemed to drift further and further to our right, always moving away from us. Each time he vanished over one of the rolling hills, it was longer until we saw him again. By the evening we had not seen the vehicle in some time and we would not see it again.

One of our vehicles got stuck and we tried to call the Badia officer for help, but to no avail. The following morning the Badia officer contacted the Jordanian Army officer by cell phone to check on us; we did not see him. I envisioned him calling us from his home.

This Badia officer owed us no loyalty. None of us in the group was related to him. We had no friendship through which we could claim rights to his hospitality, and he had been offended by his initial chastisement. Additionally, he had planned on going home to his family. Much more important.

Finally, from our conversations he had understood that we knew where we were going and that his presence was unnecessary.

## Way of Thinking
### Americans: Linear

The greatest single example of US linear thinking is the timeline and the "way ahead" charts that seem to percolate through most corporations and military units. During my time in Iraq these charts were ubiquitous. Every project had such a chart attached. The timelines all were oriented from lower left to upper right, as if to say without words that the very advancement of time itself was upward progress.

### Arabs: Network or Web

Arabs do not necessarily think in terms of timelines. Some of this has to do with aversions to planning, which will be discussed later. In my experience Arabs tend to look at projects and events as ways to create, develop, and enhance relationships. It is about developing the network.

## Purpose of Communication
### Americans: Communicate for a Purpose

This topic will be discussed in greater detail later. Here I just want to say that in US military and business circles, we have meetings and speak to move things forward, to achieve something. I have met many officers who will not speak to a counterpart if they know he or she will not budge on an issue, as they see no need to waste time in what is certain to be a fruitless discussion.

### Arabs: Communicate to Communicate

This will also be discussed later. The Arab council is about everyone having their say. I have been in meetings in which everyone spoke and almost everyone said the same thing. Repeating what had been previously stated was not viewed as redundant or wasteful, as it allowed each to speak their mind. Everyone gets to speak even if there will be no agreement. This attitude makes US policy regarding whom we do or do not speak with incomprehensible to the average Arab. You should allow everyone to express their opinion. This behavior does not include a requirement to accept or act upon everything spoken. Regardless of intent to act, everyone still gets to have their say.

## Perspective
### *Americans: Map Perspective*

Maps create artificial order. A map is a representation of the world on a two-dimensional plane, with hills, valleys, and cities all rendered in a neat and orderly set of lines and blocks. This does not reflect reality. From this order the reader can see a conceptualization from which he or she may select a navigational path. It works, and people are able to get from one place to another.

The key is the artificiality of the map. It is not reality. The very use of the term "road map" in terms of plans of action tend to communicate a similar sense of the conceptual over the concrete and real.

This rendering creates the perception that control is possible, chaos can be ordered, and one can be an instrument in eliminating that portion of chaos within one's span of control. Order can be imposed, and I am the agent of change.

### *Arabs: Street-Level Perspective*

The world is chaos. The street is chaos. This is especially true if one has ever driven in Cairo or Damascus. The world comes at one in the form of other cars, pedestrians, donkeys, sheep, slow-moving and overpacked trucks, overburdened motorcycles, debris, and road hazards like potholes. There is a cacophony of distracting sights and sounds.

This kind of worldview leads to a perspective in which plans are irrelevant, unnecessary, and often overtaken by real events. One may think one can arrive at a destination in fifteen minutes, but what if a truck is stopped and is unloading its cargo in the middle of the street? Now the trip takes one and a half hours.

Such a perspective causes one to feel either very frustrated by the lack of control or to go through life without the intention of imposing one's own control on an uncontrollable and very chaotic world. Who can control chaos? Only God. Not man, and definitely not me.

These are brief, yet important looks into how a bee and a spider will look at the same things. Again I refer the reader to the warnings at the beginning of this book. Not all Americans or all Arabs fit this simple analogy perfectly or even mostly. Many do fit many of these characteristics and this provides a way to begin questioning one's own thinking and then understanding the thinking of others.

# Examples—The Icons of Bees and Spiders: Cowboys and Bedouins

This is a brief note about icons in societies. Americans and Arabs have their own respective icon that personifies the culture. Settling on a single icon for America is difficult, as the US is a widely varied collection of immigrants and natives. I suggest that the US icon is the cowboy. By this I mean the cowboy as demonstrated in the morality plays of the American Western movie and often enacted by John Wayne. The Arab icon is much easier, as they tend to draw their historical and cultural roots from the same sources. This icon is the bedouin—probably the bedouin warrior, depending on the instance or individual. As I warned earlier this is not a comprehensive cultural survey or discussion, and because of this I will only briefly relate why these icons are useful in understanding what will be shared later in this book.

First, I want to briefly discuss the cowboy. Please remember there is a significant aspect of this icon that is Hollywood generated and has little connection to historic reality. To Americans the cowboy represents the ideal of rugged individualism. Cowboys are self-sufficient, responsible for their own welfare. They respect and honor those who are also rugged and capable. They will help and assist those in need who demonstrate these mutual characteristics. The cowboy has a sense of moral clarity that allows laws and legality to be subordinated to the individual needs of current circumstances. They take the law into their own hands and take action to ensure the law is enacted. There is an element of violence in the cowboy. All of this reflects the combination of fiction and reality. To some degree the cowboy is both a positive and a negative icon.

However, in reality, the cowboy was often ignorant of the world—his world was THE world. He was also typically uneducated, suffered from poor medical care and hygiene, and was a thorn in the side of farmers and to some degree the spread and growth of civilization.

Now I will discuss the bedouin. The bedouin is a nomad from an extremely hostile and lethal climate. Every bedouin, man and woman, knows that but for God's will and the assistance of their family or others they would perish. In such an environment one must be brave and courageous. Understanding the dangers of the environment and their reliance on the assistance of others created a tremendous sense of hospitality and generosity. Their survival might depend on help from another person, family, or tribe. They are a society of collective—the group is their security. In this collective the concept of personal property carries a looser definition than it does for those who live in settled environments with fences and doors with locks. An individual bedouin possesses little. One thing only is certain to be theirs: honor. It is possible that a bedouin man may also claim possession of a weapon and his wife, but little else. Those other things are as much owned by the family as themselves. In this loose sense of ownership a bedouin will see any unsecured item as open and available for him to take possession of. As with the cowboy, the bedouin is viewed in both a positive and a negative light. Some will say that bedouins are thieves, as they will take anything they find. Others will call them backward.

I want to address two items that I will discuss in greater detail later in this book. One relates to the harsh climate of the desert. The bedouin lives in a world of scarcity and views the whole world through this lens. A second point is that the harsh climate leads one to a pragmatic view of the world. The bedouin is intensely pragmatic—if it works the bedouin will do it, use it, adopt it, make it his own. If it does not work or does not seem to work, then he will not embrace or accept it.

I will repeatedly go back to the bedouin as the root of Arab culture. This is true. Remember my warning that there is not a single Arab world. In some parts of the Arab world there has been a great separation from the days of the bedouin. Egypt, Iraq, and Palestine are places where the bedouin traditions have less pull and significance than in others. That said, bedouin roots are still there if for no other reason than the prophet Mohammad was a bedouin and Islam's roots are bedouin. I would argue that most families in the three countries I mentioned and others that I have not still have roots that go back to a bedouin tribe and bedouin customs and courtesies.

Now we will move to some specific examples of ways bees and spiders see the world from different perspectives.

# Example #1
# Grocer vs. Provider

---

*100% satisfaction guaranteed.*

—Common marketing quote

I address the spider perspective here from a relatively extreme position of a bedouin. Bedouins typically have a relatively narrow definition of honorable work. Being a grocer (or running any businesses for that matter) is not honorable. Why? Think about a grocer from the perspective of a nomadic warrior. A grocer takes orders and he fills them. He does not hold those values held by the bedouin—such as hospitality—but is simply a servant for pay.

A provider, on the other hand, is one who provides resources as an act of hospitality or generosity. He is a source of resources, and his offers make and build connections. Not so with a grocer. A grocer, as an order filler, does not foster relationship connections. The grocer is doing what he does for monetary gain.

The following example is not in reference to a specific event, but is based on discussions and references to similar events that I heard on several occasions in 2005 and later.

Imagine a US military company commander who has recently arrived to his assigned area of operations in Iraq or elsewhere in the Arab world. The young commander is trying to put into action his cultural training. He has been told to develop relationships, so he meets with each of the village leaders in his area. In these meetings he asks what the village leader needs and makes offers of assistance based on the resources that he knows he has available. He has been taught to not make promises on which he cannot deliver. The commander walks away from the meetings with a significant list that he begins immediately to work on. Over the next several weeks and months he accomplishes a great deal of the tasks on the list. He maintains regular meetings with the village leaders. In one such meeting a village leader brings up a specific issue that the commander has failed to deliver on. He harangues the young commander for nearly an hour. The commander leaves the meeting bewildered. He cannot understand why he did not receive praise. He delivered more than 90 percent of the items requested, but still he is getting lectured on his failures and his integrity has been questioned.

This seems very unreasonable to most Americans. Where is the gratitude? Where is the appreciation? Where is this relationship that was promised by the cultural "experts"?

Imagine one's feelings when one orders online. One places an order for ten items, and nine are delivered. Is the customer happy with a 90 percent delivery rate? Absolutely not. There are complaints and requests for the items to be shipped immediately. Why? The customer in this case made a contract with the company for total delivery, not a best effort. This is a grocer–customer relationship. When one places an order with a grocer, the expectation is that the order is fully filled. No one gushes with praise when a grocer properly or accurately fills an order. It is expected. It is even required if the relationship is to be maintained.

I worked closely with foreign military sales (FMS) cases when I first arrived in Iraq in the late summer of 2010. I continued to observe the process over the entire year I was present, at times at the highest levels. I watched as Iraqi officials complained about delivery times, delays, and what they saw as poor-quality equipment. Most of these complaints were about items that were "gifts" from the United States government to the Iraqi military and security forces. They were complaining about free things! How could this be? The reason is simple. The US leaders, just like the young captain described above, made themselves grocers. They were delivering on orders, and the orders were not as promised. In some cases this was a result of the promises being difficult to keep. In other cases it was the result of miscommunication. In yet other instances it was a result of the desire on the part of the Iraqi to put the American squarely in the role of the grocer and make sure the American understood that.

It is unfortunate that the US handles foreign military sales by placing its executors in the role of grocer filling out shopping lists and then delivering on the requests. From the American perspective an honest grocer is not just honorable, but a respected member of the community. Those who achieve in business are among the most respected people in society. Many of the officers with whom I have worked and who have tremendous experience with the US foreign military sales program say that the reason so many countries want to participate in the program is because we do deliver in a corruption-free environment. Some of the very things that make foreign military sales slow and cumbersome are there to make sure that crony capitalism and corruption do not play a role. Are these experienced men and women correct? Is the US system for foreign military sales and foreign aid respected? I think the answer is complex, but the gist is that those from other countries who have experience with US business culture do understand and appreciate the transparency and corruption-free environment. Those with less experience see the grocer and want the 100% satisfaction guarantee.

Clearly there is an impasse. Or is there?

How is this done successfully among the spiders? By being a provider. The difference between grocer and provider is not overwhelming. It is mainly a difference of nuance. Please remember the section on the fact that we are different—nuances count! I will provide an example to illustrate what I mean by this.

I accompanied my Jordanian battalion commander on a visit to one of the Jordanian military regional commands. The battalion in which I served was responsible for operating and maintaining thermal cameras and other surveillance devices on the Jordanian border. The military regions provided the infantry and other resources, but the cameras and those who operated them were ours. When a camera went down we repaired it in our battalion workshop or sent it back to the company if more extensive repairs were needed. On this visit we were transporting two recently repaired cameras that had come from this region in the commander's vehicle. The military regional commander was a promotable one-star general equivalent (soon to be a two-star general equivalent).

We were invited into the office. The entire meeting lasted more than an hour. The first forty minutes or so were dedicated to the standard Arabic pleasantries of greetings, coffee, discussion of family, the status of the battalion, and life as a commander (my battalion commander had only assumed command a few weeks earlier). The regional commander expressed concerns over the general challenges of protecting the border and the specific geographic challenges of his region. The meeting seemed to be going nowhere, and it was moving slowly at that. This is because I did not recognize the web strands being cast out and strengthened. About forty minutes into the meeting the battalion commander began a discussion on one of the soldiers in the battalion and the medical needs of one of his parents.

A brief note on Jordanian military benefits is in order. When a Jordanian joins the military he and his parents receive free medical care. The Jordanian military hospitals are among the best in the country when it comes to caring for the average citizen. This is a substantial benefit for the average soldier. This said, there are ways to ensure that your needs are met more quickly than is otherwise usual. A letter from a senior ranking military leader will help speed the process.

My commander laid out the needs of the soldier's parent and expressed the benefits of a letter from the regional commander. In almost the next breath my commander shared that we had two recently repaired cameras in the back of his vehicle and that the region would benefit from having these cameras on the border.

I was stunned. From a US perspective these cameras belonged to the region. They had only been returned to the battalion for maintenance, and yet my commander seemed to use them as his own chips with which he could bargain.

The regional commander took no offense. He took it in stride. He said that he would be honored to provide the letter to help the soldier and his family, and my commander said he would be happy to provide the cameras to aid the regional commander in defense of the kingdom.

I walked out realizing that I had witnessed something profound.

In a later event I was called into the battalion commander's office and chastised for sharing information about newly received, recently repaired cameras from the manufacturer. The previous afternoon I had been at the airport inventorying the shipment and verifying serial numbers. I called the commander from the airport to confirm the arrival and the numbers of cameras received. I called the supplier to provide the same information. I called no one else. I had shared no such information outside these two calls, but my commander had been contacted that morning by another regional commander who had heard there were cameras at the battalion and wanted more for his area of responsibility. I was ordered by my commander to not ever reveal the number of cameras ready for issue. This was to be shared only with him, and then with his permission to the higher headquarters. This was the only time I had seen the commander angry with me. My assurances that I had complied with his direction and hadn't shared the information with anyone outside the battalion did little to console him. I am not sure if he ever believed me on this point.

I also walked out of this meeting realizing I had experienced something profound. It took me a long while to put the pieces of both events together.

What I had witnessed was what it meant to be a provider. In the first story, both men were providers. They both responded to the needs of the other and both looked generous. Both received a resource they desired and both provided a resource the other could not provide themselves. This was an Arab win-win situation. In the second situation my commander was upset because someone had provided information to another that allowed them to put him in the position of a grocer—an order was made and he needed to fill it. Principles of hospitality meant that he could not refuse the request. He was stuck. He was no longer a provider.

The differences are very slight. In both cases my commander provided the same resource to a regional commander. In one case it was an offer from him and in the other it was a request to fill an order. In one case he was the provider and in the other case he was a grocer. To be a provider is best.

The US could follow a similar pattern in how it makes offers. After one of the seminars I delivered on this topic in Iraq, a woman approached me to share a story about her time working as a staffer on Capitol Hill. She told me about the manner of negotiations between members of the House of Representatives or the Senate with respect to a piece of legislation. In her experience those negotiations were similar to the provider example shared above. At the highest levels in the US government and military it seems that everyone wants to be a provider, and most work very hard to avoid having orders placed that they have to fill.

Being a provider gives one greater credibility and influence. The provider hooks someone up. It is not impossible for the US and US officials to be providers. It requires a conscious understanding of what is being offered, how, and why.

# Example #2
# Follow the Politics vs.
# Follow the Money

One of the classic lines that cross from reality to film and back again is from the movie *All the President's Men,* when the informant whispers in the parking garage, "Follow the money." It is iconic in that it encapsulates the nature of US conspiracy culture in a few words.

During the 2007 Asia Cup for soccer I had a conversation with a fellow Jordanian officer. This officer explained how he believed that Iraq would win the cup championship that year. Not really understanding the teams and their relative strengths I asked why he thought that was so. He stated that Iraq would win because it was in the interest of the United States and other "powerful countries" for Iraq to win, as celebrating a major sports victory would bring calm to Iraq and the Iraqi people. He further explained that one needed to "follow the politics" to understand conspiracies.

I was staggered by his use of the phrase, and I explained to him the line from *All the President's Men.* He stated that in the Middle East, it is through political benefit that conspiracies are tracked. Incidentally, Iraq did win the Asia Cup in 2007.

This different view of the motivation for conspiracy and corruption is also related to the next example—*Definition of Success: Position vs. Progress.*

When one reflects on this difference—following the money or the politics—then the conspiracy theories regarding the cause or source of the attacks of September 11, 2001 become clearer. I was an instructor of international students from Saudi Arabia and Jordan in Fort Knox at the time of the attacks. Immediately following the attacks my US students and I were tasked to go to the post headquarters to help with the emergency operations of the post. After several days of chaotic service at the post level I returned to my duties as an instructor and was reunited with my Arab students.

These two dedicated Muslims tried to explain what they understood. It was an education I was not prepared to receive. I understand much better now. What they were reading within days of the attack was predominantly centered on two main theories. One, the Israelis did it. Two, the US government did it.

From a US follow-the-money perspective, this seems ludicrous. What US president would destroy the national economy simply to start a Christian–Muslim war? Contrary to the most ardent critics of President Bush, no president would order such a thing. The same could be said about Israel—they would not destroy the economy of their strongest supporter. From a US-based conspiracy theory perspective, these ideas are just plain crazy.

From a follow-the-politics perspective, these theories make sense. Who benefits politically from a war between the Christian West and the Muslim Middle East? Clearly it is Israel. Whose presidency gained immediate support domestically and internationally? The US president's.

The Middle East is a region dominated by leaders who are above the will of the people. In most cases public criticism of those leaders is against the law, and violating the law incurs severe penalties, usually prison. When a snippet of news comes out that implies criticism of the leadership, the general population assumes this is only the tip of the iceberg, so to speak, and that there is so much more they aren't being told. Conspiracy theories fill in the missing parts. These theories provide, at times, plausible explanations for events and decisions that the news does not and cannot provide.

This same skepticism is applied to news reports from the Western media as well. When a report comes to the region from a Western source that criticizes the US president, the assumption is again that this is only the very tip. They assume that the Western press functions under the same legal and punitive restrictions as their own media. As a result the conspiracy theories of Western behavior are huge, as this behavior must be more extreme than the reported reality. This is true of the average taxi driver and man on the street.

I know people in the Middle Eastern media who have friends in the Western press and understand the differences between Western and Middle Eastern media, but the average person living in the Middle East does not. The average person assumes a link between media establishments and government. This is usually true throughout the Middle East, where much of the media is state-run or at least state-sanctioned or approved. It is partly for this reason that protests can be so severe when a Western newspaper or television program criticizes Islam. The assumption of the people on the street is that the program or article is not simply the statement of belief of one individual or media outlet. It is rather a quasi-official statement of national belief or policy.

Those who dismiss conspiracy theories coming from the Middle East miss the benefit these theories provide in understanding the thinking of the people in this region. People do not think things because they are stupid. It is rather to the contrary—they do so because they are intelligent. They may be ignorant of facts and details, but they are not stupid. It is both useful and important to understand and empathize with the perspective of the various theories so that one can move toward a greater sense of total empathy.

# Example #3
# Definition of Success:
# Position vs. Progress

I remember a briefing I received as a young lieutenant in 1993 in which the topic of Saddam Hussein came up. The commander stated that he would leave Saddam in power, because once you've whipped someone that bad they will never forget it. He may be a bad man, but he is now a bad man who understands his place. Or words to that effect. This general view of Desert Storm—that the US was the victor—was pervasive in the 1990s.

In the Arab world the view was different. By 1993 both George H. W. Bush and Margaret Thatcher had been voted out of office, yet Saddam was still in power. From a Middle East perspective, this meant that Saddam was the winner. The longer US planes flew over Iraq and Saddam continued to defy them by firing back, the more he made clear that he was the winner. In the US the news blamed Saddam for the bad situation in Iraq resulting from sanctions—he was bringing suffering on his people. Throughout most of the Arab world the suffering of the Iraqi people was viewed as the fault of the US and the West.

Another difference in perspective relates to Yasser Arafat, the longtime leader of the Palestine Liberation Organization. I cannot recall all the criticism I have heard about him from US media sources. So many US government officials and news pundits have asserted over and over again that he hurt his people through his positions and behavior. It has been said that the Palestinian people were worse off after his service ended then before it began. The outpouring of genuine affection toward him on his death communicated the respect and admiration felt for him from his people and throughout the Arab world. Why? Because he maintained his position. He died in power.

In the US and the West, among *bees,* the prevailing attitude is that a leader brings progress to his people and his country, and if the leader cannot or does not do so, that leader is removed from office or simply regarded as a failure. In the Arab world, among *spiders*, the view is that the leader needs to retain his position to be successful, and any leader who is still in position is a success.

The Arab view of leadership success was clearly demonstrated during the Arab Spring of 2011. If one recalls the way the movement began in the various countries, then one can see that the initial call was for more freedoms for the people. The people soon began to call for the removal of the leader, and that is where the focus of the protests remained until the leaders were removed. It really was about taking the *spider* from the center of his web. This was true in every case—Tunisia, Libya, Egypt, Yemen, Bahrain, Syria, Jordan.

In the movie *Lawrence of Arabia,* the character of the sheikh of the Howeitat tribe, played by Anthony Quinn, steps to the edge of his tent, gestures in grandiose fashion to those seated beyond it, and says, "I am poor, because I am a river to my people." The people cheer at this bold statement that is both true and not. The movie character meant that through him flowed the benefits and material wealth of his tribe. To a bedouin there are very few things on earth more amazing and important than a river. Water is the source of life, and where rivers flow, life blossoms and thrives.

Yasser Arafat died a man of tremendous wealth, and yet he lived a simple life for the most part among his people. He used a lot of the money gained by and donated to him as a means to be *a river to his people*, as did the fictional film character. This river brings benefits and progress at times, but progress is not necessarily the purpose. The purpose is to be and continue to be the river: to bring benefits and generosity to those for whom the leader has responsibility.

It is important to recognize that there are differences within this paradigm. Some of the countries of the Arab world have demonstrated tremendous material and political progress. Progress is not bad. Arabs want progress and development. The point is that progress in and of itself is not the standard and sole definition of leadership success within Arab culture.

Leadership is the gaining and holding of the position. To have a defined course for the river, so to speak. Leaders provide benefits, but more importantly, they endure.

# Example #4
# Evil Genius vs. Naive Bungler:
# Which Is Preferred?

In the fall of 2010 I sat in an office within the Iraqi Ministry of Defense and spoke with several of the employees there. It was a casual conversation intended to build my own web connections within this new environment.

As is often the case the topic of the conversation turned toward politics. One of the Iraqi men present, who had property in the US and who thought he was very familiar with US policies and politics, stated some opinions regarding the sitting US president and his interests regarding the Arab people, particularly the people of Iraq. His opinion was that the president wanted the Iraqi people to suffer and be divided. He thought US policy was purposely designed to achieve this. The statements of the president to the contrary were intended as deception to further keep the Arab people off-balance and divided. The unstated thought was why else would the US do so many things that caused suffering and hardship in the Arab world—subjugation of the Palestinian people, chaos and difficulties in Iraq, support of dictatorial Arab leaders.

This was not the first time I had heard this sort of theory. I had come to expect it. I sought to address the theory in an indirect correction. I offered that the US president wanted exactly what he said. He genuinely wanted the Arab people to enjoy the blessings and benefits of modern democracy, economic growth and prosperity, and freedom. I stated that even the president of the United States does not have perfect knowledge and understanding of the complex issues around the world. He only knows what he is told by his advisors and experts, and sometimes mistakes are made.

My statements are rather tame in most American circles. The idea that the US president does not have perfect understanding of the world is not radical. That said, as I made these statements I observed the look, expressions, and body language of my Iraqi associates. They became more and more uncomfortable with my statements. By the time I ended they were visibly shaken and at complete disagreement with my radical and unacceptable pronouncements.

What I came to understand through this simple exchange and many others that I have had in similar circumstances is that the idea of the most powerful leader in the world being a Dudley Do-Right character—seeking good, but sometimes being a naive bungler[11]—was completely unacceptable. These Iraqi participants and many other Arabs with whom I have had these conversations were and are more comfortable with the image of the president of the US as an evil genius working through a variety of complex and secret machinations to oppress and overwhelm the Arabs. The evil genius who prepares diabolical plans and who achieves bad things through intent is more comforting than a good-hearted leader who causes bad things through bad luck,

[11] I want to emphasize that the use of the phrase "naive bungler" is given as a polemical statement to show an extreme and not as a statement of criticism of the president of the United States. As I have served as a military diplomat I always try to portray the US leadership in the best light possible and to communicate the complexities of US policy and politics. For those who think explaining US–Middle East policy is easy, I challenge you to take a cab ride in any Middle Eastern capital and discuss this with the driver for forty-five minutes.

incompetence of execution, or simply the exigencies of the law of unintended consequences.

Once again this view is not universal, but it is common and even prevalent on the Arab street. Converse with any taxi driver or barber in Amman, Cairo, Baghdad, Rabat, Tunis, or Damascus, and you will hear that George Bush or Barack Obama intended the bad things that have happened to the Arabs. They will not accept that these things have been the consequences of complex dynamics resulting from imperfect information, understanding, and execution.

# Example #5
# Communication:
# Explicit vs. Implicit

Maybe the biggest difference between US and Arabic cultures is language. The most obvious difference is that English is read left to right and Arabic is read right to left. Later in this book, I will address the importance of understanding Arabic language in developing greater empathy and influence. Here I will discuss the nature of communication in each language—English is purpose-built for direct and explicit communication, whereas Arabic is a poetic and implicit language.

There is not sufficient space here to have a complex linguistic discussion, but in brief, modern English began as a language of nonnative speakers. This process may have begun before the Norman conquest of England in 1066, but it definitely increased in pace afterward. English does not have case endings and does not have gender for inanimate objects like chairs or cars or sandwiches. These are things that Old English had and modern English does not. These are also attributes that make languages more difficult for a nonnative to learn. English went through changes as many nonnatives learned it and picked up vocabulary from many other languages. This extra vocabulary in some part added to the specificity of the language. The current version of English is very precise. The volume of vocabulary provides plenty of options for precision.

English is not the native language of ancient religion. It is rather a language to which those religious languages have been translated. Translation usually brings a greater aspect of rationality and pragmatism. Poetry is not always lost, but translated texts inevitably lose the impact of the native flow, pacing, rhyme, and rhythm.

Arabic is a language that maintained a fixed point of reference—the Koran—for more than 1,400 years. The fixed point provides constancy. Arabic is a language of nomadic tribes. It seems that when modern scholars compiled dictionaries of modern Arabic, words were taken from each of the tribes, and thus we have numerous words for lion, sand, storm, fire (and its attendant parts), and only one for snow and ice combined. This makes sense coming from a desert people.

Arabic is a poetic language. One can hear the poetry in Koranic readings. The sounds of the language have a natural rhyme that makes it beautiful even if not understood. I am not sure if the poetic nature of the language gave rise to a culture of poetry, or if the culture of poetry made the language sound more poetic.

Arabic is not simply the native language of the religion of Islam. In the mind of Muslims and the teachings of Islam, Arabic is the language of God. God has a language, and it is Arabic. It is for this reason that there is no translation of the Koran from Arabic. All such Korans are interpretations of God's language into another language. For this reason Arabic is viewed as difficult, challenging, complex, and poetic. To learn the language of God is not supposed to be easy or simple. The prophet Mohammed taught that each verse in the Koran has multiple meanings, the highest of which is known only to God, bringing yet another understanding of the poetic nature and communicative intent of Arabic. Direct and simple communication is for the child and not the adult.

The precision of modern English and the poetic nature
of Arabic run in stark contrast to each other. This provides
additional challenges, as the two languages are sometimes
spoken for different reasons or purposes. Americans typically
speak to make a point, whereas Arabs often speak to hear the
language spoken. Such a difference leads to the difference of
explicit versus implicit communication.

The accompanying graphics communicate this difference.
When an American speaks, he or she is trying to make a point.
An American would define a square in direct words and phrases,
as four sides of exactly the same lengths that meet at four right
angles. That is a square explicitly defined.

An Arab might describe the square in the sense of a void
surrounded by an area of definition. The bounded void has a
shape with equal dimensions. The explanation of the shape is
implied, as shown through the illustrations.

In both cases a square is described, yet the path to arrive at
this definition is very different.

I have repeatedly sat in meetings in which an American spoke
in the direct language of Americans and then an Arab spoke. The
Arab spent time in poetic greetings and then thanked the visitor
in multiple ways with a variety of phrases. As he moved to the
topic at hand he addressed the issue as in the case of the defined
square—by moving around the primary point of discussion,
touching on it, but not ever explicitly defining it. It was for the
listener to divine the meaning of the words. In most cases the
speaker does not mean to cause difficulty; rather, the speaker's
intent is to express himself as an educated and urbane speaker
of Arabic. I have met many Arab men who seem to simply take
joy in their language; they love to hear it spoken and to hear the
words come out of their own mouths. They are not speaking just
to make a point, but to have joy in the glory of God's language

spoken well.

I heard stories in the Jordanian Army of times when King Hussein would address the army. It was told that his mastery of Arabic was so great that men wept at the beauty of it.

My family and I attended a Christian church in Jordan that had local Jordanian members as well as expatriate members. Everything was spoken and then translated either from Arabic to English or vice versa, depending on the speaker. When an Arab would speak, my wife and I would try to understand the point they were trying to make. Later I came to understand what I have been explaining—they were speaking in a poetic style that required a tremendous amount of divination to see the square, as it were.

The fact that speaking has different purposes means that there are different rules about it. Americans tend to view meetings in terms of a law of time conservation: time wasted is money lost, and therefore meetings that do not produce a result are wasted efforts. Americans do not want to have meetings for the sake of meeting. This is also true if a point of view is strong and known. If it is known that their counterpart will not agree with their opinion, then Americans will not have a meeting just to waste time in an irresolvable discussion. In Arab culture everyone gets to speak regardless of agreement or consensus.

I remember sitting in a meeting in the city of Ma'an, Jordan, where everyone around the table spoke in introduction. With only slight variations, they all spoke the same words, said the same sentences, made the same points. An American would typically see this as a wasted forty minutes or so, but the Arabs understood they all had a right to make those remarks regardless of who else had said them.

Think about how it looks to the average Arab when the US government refuses to meet with a group or nation simply because

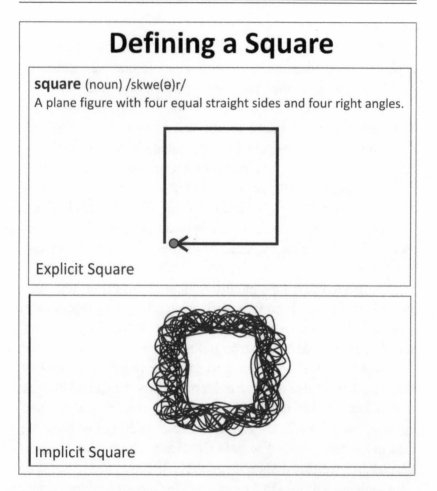

# Defining a Square

**square** (noun) /skwe(ə)r/
A plane figure with four equal straight sides and four right angles.

Explicit Square

Implicit Square

there is a preconceived or even clearly understood disagreement and no hope of agreement. This is rude behavior. By denying the other side a voice, something fundamental to the culture and thinking of the people is being denied, not unlike a US view on denying life, liberty, and the pursuit of happiness.

If democracy is defined as having the opportunity to speak your mind (incidentally, this was a common definition provided to me by Israelis), then Arabs have a strong and innate sense of democratic values.

I do not want to let the poetic nature of this discussion cloud the fact that speaking one's mind and having one's views accepted and implemented are not the same thing. Many Arab leaders will allow people to speak knowing that they will never implement or act upon the words of those speaking. Still the voice is allowed to be heard.

One final example. I sat in the Jordanian battalion commander's office and one of the soldiers (a US private equivalent in rank) was called in to receive a punishment for being absent from duty without leave. After the commander pronounced judgment, he allowed the soldier to speak. The soldier pleaded his case about the challenges of his family—all the things that he had previously said when the case was first laid before the commander—and argued against the hard and unbending army policies. The commander let him rail against both himself and the army. This does not happen in the US Army. A soldier has their opportunity to speak, and once that opportunity is passed, then they are to accept the verdict without further comment, and certainly without lengthy condemnations of leadership and policies. In this case the voiced complaints had no weight on the decision. That seemed typical, but a bedouin gets to speak and his voice should be heard.

# Example #6
# Preventive Maintenance:
# Rich Culture and Poor Culture

This example is the least culturally specific. This is not simply an Arab–American difference or a bee–spider difference. This is a really a rich culture–poor culture issue. That said, it is a critical difference to consider and understand.

Reflect on why one sees preventative maintenance as a good thing. One who believes in conducting preventative maintenance believes that by paying a nominal amount in parts, fluids, and labor on a regular basis, they can prevent a catastrophic payment later. A specific example is the oil change every three thousand miles or three months. The belief is that paying $49.99 for an oil change four times a year will prevent an engine failure that might cost thousands of dollars. The interesting part is that the vast majority of people who do this do not really know why. This is a negative proposition—by doing thing A, one prevents thing B—but it is impossible to prove a negative. One cannot know that the engine will fail if a regular oil change is not performed. Of course various companies have run tests over the years, and many engineers have written papers on the subject, but almost no one has actually read these studies. The simple thing is that people from rich cultures believe it.

This is an almost religious sense of faith in the concept. This statement gets me into a little trouble when I have engineers in my audiences. They protest that it isn't faith, and that the studies and science support the proposition. Once again the rest of us just accept the engineers' certainty as many accept a prophet's certainty. I say this as a believer myself. I regularly pay for the oil change and conduct preventative maintenance, but then again I have the money to behave in such a manner.

Preventative maintenance is for those who can afford to budget money for regular and apparently unnecessary services. The "unnecessary" is from the perspective of those who are not believers. People without money are almost categorically not believers in such a philosophy. Anyone reading this who has spent time among the poor anywhere in the world—from rural and urban America to sub-Saharan Africa—has seen how maintenance is performed in these cultures. Vehicles are used until they break. There is no need to repair a perfectly operational piece of equipment. Once the vehicle breaks, then repairs are made to gain the necessary operational capability. This is good enough maintenance. In the military we call these battlefield repairs: one gets the vehicle to operate sufficiently enough to either continue the mission or self-recover to a maintenance facility. Some of the best mechanics of this sort are in the developing world. I have watched people on the side of the road tinker with an engine until they get it running and the vehicle is able to limp forward on its way. The overall capability of the vehicle may be reduced, but the vehicle still operates and can accomplish the task needed, so therefore it is good enough.

Why do poor people do maintenance in this way? Simply because they do not have the money to do it the other way. Of course a believer will say that by doing preventative maintenance a poor person would actually save money. Though that may be true, it is not apparent. It requires belief in the system and some degree of faith. I know that my vehicle works now, so I do not *need* to repair it now. When it breaks, then I *need* to repair it. One who lives from moment to moment will not pay money that does not *need* to be spent. One does not have that luxury.

One of the biggest frustrations I have seen in discussions on cross-cultural work is communicating the importance of preventative maintenance. US equipment is fantastic. It is also complex, expensive, and maintenance intensive. When communicating these things, it is necessary to understand that a person from a poor culture will not necessarily concur with the need for such care, or if they do, then they will question whether the equipment has benefit at all.

When I first arrived in Iraq in 2010, I worked on the M1A1 main battle tank program. The US had sold a significant number of these tanks to the Iraqi Army. I spent eleven years working with this tank in the US Army and firmly believe that it is the best tank in the world, but I also know that it requires a great deal of maintenance with a lot of expensive spare parts. As I sat in meetings with Iraqi senior armor and maintenance leaders, I heard them repeatedly bemoan the costs of maintaining the tanks. They often, almost wistfully, referred to the days of the T-72 Soviet main battle tank. This is a much less maintenance-intensive tank. It is also slower, less protected, and less accurate. One of the Iraqi generals said that they did not need to do maintenance on the M1A1 tanks, as they were brand new. They could go for at least a year and a half before requiring any maintenance.

Many of the American officers in the room looked aghast, and then tried to dissuade the general of this belief. I could see on the Iraqi general's face that he was thinking less and less of this vehicle. It was almost as if I could hear him think, *This tank cannot be as good as they claim if it needs so much maintenance.*

Communicating the need for preventative maintenance is

a challenge that I will address in greater detail when I explain about walls to cross-cultural communication.

# Example #7
## Problem Solving:
## Direct Action vs. Mediation

If you have a problem with a person, then you need to confront that person and resolve the problem. Such advice is common in American culture. Even when dealing with a sensitive topic like sexual harassment, the requirement is for the harassed to confront the harasser and identify the inappropriate behavior. This is a challenge for Americans as well as anyone else, and in the sensitive area of sexual harassment, we have developed other ways to deal with such a problem. Usually that is through some form of mediation or third party.

Americans tend to cling to that cowboy philosophy of solving your own problems. In most Western morality plays, the good guy confronts the bad guy, sometimes in the middle of a dusty street, and the problem is resolved. If the confrontation is with handguns the resolution is final, but if the confrontation is with fists, as in the stereotypical bar fight, then the defeated man acknowledges the skill and determination of the victor, and both parties may actually walk away as friends or respected enemies. That is the Hollywood Western philosophy, but in many ways Americans actually encourage a similar style of direct action in their conflict resolution advice. Think on the US government leaders and Sunday talk show pundits who espouse the need for direct talks between two parties of a conflict.

Arab behavior is different in that it is extremely difficult for an Arab to admit weakness or defeat. Honor is a hallmark of the culture. Remember the earlier comment that to a bedouin, honor may be the only thing he actually considers his own. It is his self-defining characteristic. Admitting weakness affects that honor.

Among bedouin a problem is usually resolved through the mediation of a respected elder, one who hears the grievances of both sides and then makes an informed and presumably wise judgment. Throughout Arab history, judges held a particular place of respect. Judges in this context were not those who simply made judgments based on laws with mandatory sentences. They were expected to consider statements, laws, and intent and use common sense to do what was right to resolve the issue. The simple point was that if you had a problem with another person, you took this problem to a third party for mediation.

The mediator absolves both parties of shame. The final decision is not an admission by one side of fault or weakness. It is a ruling of a respected member of the community. Even if the judgment goes hard against one party, that party always has the ability to blame the final decision on someone else. The party does not admit to anything, and thus to him he retains some element of personal honor.

The best modern-day example of this is the scene that occurs at a traffic accident. Anyone who has seen a traffic accident in the Arab world can attest to the standard sequence. Two cars collide. Both drivers get out and begin direct action in accordance with the American mode of solving a problem. This typically results in high-volume yelling and finger pointing. Sometimes it even comes to blows. I once saw a man hit with a metal pole, and I once saw a driver throwing rocks at another vehicle. Then someone steps in. If this is in a small village, the intervening person may just be another civilian passerby. In a more urban setting, the intervention is usually by the police. This intervening character becomes a mediator. The mediator hears the complaints of one party and then the other. The mediator weighs what he sees and what he hears and renders a judgment. If the intervening person is a civilian, usually the civilian will make a great effort to ensure that the verdict is mutually acceptable. If the intervention is made by a police officer, the judgment will be faster and less likely to please both sides equally.

It is interesting to note that Americans also use mediation in such cases, though American mediation is done through both a present and a non-present third party: the police and the insurance company. After the accident occurs some angry words may be exchanged, but generally people behave civilly as they exchange insurance information, await a police decision, and then head back to their previous errands to the extent that they can.

US calls for direct negotiation miss both the cultural norm in the Middle East as well as American behavior in stressful situations. In the US, it is common for arbitration to solve intractable negotiations: insurance companies hash out the details of settlements, and monitors on playgrounds and referees on playing fields make sure everyone plays by the rules. Nearly every move toward peace in the Middle East has been the result of mediated negotiations, not direct negotiations: Camp David and Oslo are two such examples.

These examples show that as previously stated, the differences between Arabs and Americans regarding problem solving are not that great. There is room to understand the Arab perspective of defending personal honor.

# Example #8
# Planning vs. Will of God

*Set the conditions.*
—US military maxim for operational preparation

*In shah Allah*
—Common Arabic phrase meaning
"according to God's will" or "with God's will"

I spent three celebrations of the month of Ramadan in the Jordanian Army. This is the Islamic month[12] when Muslims fast from before sunup to after sundown. The fasting is comprehensive, as it requires the devout to go without food or drink or other physical pleasures, including smoking or sexual relations.

I have been in the Middle East for several more celebrations of Ramadan, but the ones I spent in the Jordanian Army were some of the most instructive. I worked at the battalion headquarters, where between two and three hundred soldiers were present on any given duty day. Like most Americans I had heard about and witnessed Muslims in the US who drank alcohol or indulged in other behaviors forbidden by their religion. I was curious about

---

[12] The Islamic calendar is lunar based. Each month begins with the new moon, and mid-month is the full moon. Ramadan is the ninth month in the Islamic calendar. As the calendar is solely lunar, it is not fixed to the Western or Gregorian calendar, and the months change each year with a migration of 11–12 days. Thus every thirty-three years or so the Islamic calendar will make a complete cycle of the Gregorian calendar, and Ramadan will again be in coincidence with where it started thirty-three or so years earlier.

the level of devotion or piety in their faith. I was pleasantly surprised during Ramadan, as in my service I never once saw a soldier or officer indulge in any behavior that violated his fast. I want to repeat, not once did I see a soldier or officer eat or drink or smoke (arguably the biggest challenge for some) during any of those three Ramadan months. That isn't to say that none did, but I never saw it, and it would have been difficult for them to hide it from me day after day and week after week. I was truly impressed by this practice of their faith.

One may question why I reference Ramadan observance in a section about planning and the will of God. I do so to set the stage for a discussion of overall piety. Many of the US service members with whom I have served think that religious observance among Muslims in the Middle East is something akin to going through the motions. I am certain that this may be true for some. I have known a few Muslims who questioned the practice of the details of their faith, but it has been my experience that for the vast majority of Muslims, their faith is a deep and profound part of who they are, how they see the world, and how they perceive their role in the world. Ramadan is one of the most extreme examples of this perception of religion, world, and place. One of the most common examples is the use of the phrase *in shah Allah.*[13]

Many of the Westerners I have known who have lived or served in the Middle East have a negative view of this phrase. Most hear it as a way to say "no," or as a delaying tactic. Though I can say that I have heard the phrase used in such a context, it is not how I have heard it used most often, and certainly not how it is used when spoken from one Arab to another.

The word islam[14] is an Arabic verbal noun that means

---

[13] This phrase literally means "in, with, by, or according to the will of God."

[14] Intentionally used here in lower case to connote the verbal noun and not the religion.

*submission.* In the case of the religion Islam, it means submission to the will of God: the acknowledgment that God's will is superior to and of greater importance than one's own. A muslim is one who has made the submission or acknowledgment that the one and only God is the God to whom they submit their will. This meaning is profound, and just to call oneself Muslim carries a powerful connotation. Thus when any Muslim worthy to hold that title makes any statement of intent such as "tomorrow I **will** go to the market," that statement must be followed by "*in shah Allah.*" In this case, *in shah Allah* is a benediction asking for God's blessing and concurrence with the statement. To do otherwise would be supremely presumptuous—to place one's own will above that of God's. I have found this phrase to be profoundly pious.

As stated above, there are those who have used the phrase with Westerners as a way of saying "no" or to imply they will give less than their best effort. Those who use the phrase to connote something less than their best effort unfortunately do so as a result of their association with Westerners who demand statements of intent regularly. I have met many Muslims who will jokingly use the phrase to mean something similar to "when a pig flies." This is not an indication of a lack of piety, but simply the presence of a sense of humor.

Intentionality is a bee behavior. It is about planning and a focus on tasks. One who sees the world from the street perspective and accepts the world as a place of chaos over which they have very little or no control, does not really believe that their intentions have much impact on their own life. Therefore, such people, the spiders of this book, are not inclined to make statements that bind them to an impossibility. Will they be at the event tomorrow at a precise time? The vagaries of traffic, accidents, the whims of family and friends, the wishes of a boss, and simply the challenges of life all conspire against such certainty. Will they? Only if God so wills it, as He is the only one with the power to make it happen.

The US military lives on the idea of creating conditions for success. In planning for conventional military operations, the intent is to shape the battlefield, cause one's opponent to go to a certain location, or do a certain thing that will enable a friendly action or event. This is a world of intentionality: the battle unfolds as one chooses because one has shaped it to be so. The idea of shaping relates to will. The US military and others talk about imposing their will on the enemy. Great commanders are viewed as great because they were able to impose their will and make things occur as they so choose.

Many reading this might ask about the German military theoretician Carl von Clausewitz, who emphasized the unexpected events that can happen in *the fog of war*. Retired US general Colin Powell has many times talked about the maxim that *no plan survives first contact with the enemy*. If this is true, then why plan at all? This is the questions my armor school students often asked me. This is not a book about military tactics so I will not answer such a question, but these seeming contradictions are interesting to note when talking about the cross-cultural dynamic.

The Western military mind acknowledges that planning may be irrelevant because the enemy *has a vote*. However, the same mind believes that it must conduct detailed analysis and planning. The more detailed the planning, the better things will be understood, and the better prepared the commander and subordinate units will be in executing the mission. I am of this mind-set, and therefore some of the suggestions in this book will discuss setting conditions and shaping engagements to ensure greater success. I am a bee, but I am a bee who sees what the spider sees as well.

The conflict comes when a Westerner demands of an Arab to plan and demonstrate intentionality, to shape the battlefield or whatever field of competition or interaction in which the parties may be involved. To do so may be tantamount to heresy to a devout Muslim.

As I wrote this book I lived in the United Arab Emirates, where a great many devout Muslims have demonstrated that it is possible to plan and to still acknowledge God's will. The Emirati leadership grasps both parts and is meshing them together. The challenge is how one communicates this to a more conventionally minded counterpart. Even in the United Arab Emirates, some officers balk at doing predictive analysis. As one said to me when I asked in 2011 for a prediction of the number of students who would attend a school in the upcoming year of 2012, "2010 I can tell you about, but 2012 only God knows."

# Example #9
# Change: Understanding Time, Perception of Law, and Flexibility

*And he gave unto Moses, when he had made an end of communing with him upon mount Sinai, two tables of testimony, tables of stone, written with the*

*finger of God.*

—Exodus 31:18 (King James Version)

The very image of the finger of God writing the Ten Commandments in stone conveys the idea of permanence. This idea has pervaded Western culture, particularly American culture. *Written in stone* is a common phrase used to denote something immutable and definite. I believe this initial concept of a permanent law has shaped Western thinking with regard to rule of law. There are lines that should not and cannot be crossed. Change in some things is a violation of the law. Not only is this attitude apparent regarding religious edict, it is also evident when one contemplates how US political and civic leaders talk about the constitution as if it were also written in stone.

Another image of permanence, one I will use to contrast the Western and Arab cultural perceptions of the concepts discussed in this section, is the mountain versus the sand dune.

In the West, the mountain is an image of permanence. It is immovable and slow to change. The Western conception of law is that the law is the law: it is fixed and applies to everyone. Contracts are fixed documents with set terms. These ideas of finality and set boundaries affect how we do business. There is little flexibility for an individual, even a senior leader, to adjust the terms of the contract or the law. Such adjustments—to move the mountain, as it were—require the voice of the people, the work of lawyers and judges, or the efforts of some other collective body. The climbing of the mountain is a linear progression, a nonstop ascent. Progress must move things forward and up. It is expected that all leaders move things forward and advance the status of the people. The next generation should and will have better lives than those of the preceding generation.

Arab culture has a different iconic image in such circumstances. It is that of a sand dune. Sand dunes can be enormous, even hundreds of feet high, and contain thousands of tons of sand. They are never permanent. Even the largest sand dunes will change over time. They may change slowly or quite rapidly in the face of a fierce storm. A sand dune can even disappear entirely and become part of a flattened landscape. Such an iconic construct leads to a very different sense of permanence. Nothing is permanent. Let me give an example.

While in Jordan, my son and I participated in the Boy Scouts of America. For one of the campouts we planned to camp in a national forest. One of the other fathers, a native Jordanian with dual US–Jordanian citizenship, coordinated the arrangements for this outing with the warden responsible for that particular forest. When we all arrived, the man in question was not present. Instead, his cousin was watching the forest for him. His cousin, not having been informed of our arrival, was surprised and said we needed to leave. We had not followed the proper procedures to be granted permission to camp. The father who made the earlier negotiations spoke with the cousin and then called the forest warden. They spoke on the phone for several minutes. The cousin and his assistant were friendly throughout. The father passed the phone to the cousin. The cousin spoke for a few moments with the warden and then smiled and said everything was okay. We could stay. I have camped and hiked in many parts of the US and in several countries in the Middle East. The US has, by far, the most rules. If a US forest or park warden had said that we needed to leave, there would have been no argument, no discussion, no possibility of talking him or her into a different decision. We would have left. In Arab countries everything is open for negotiations.

When my family and I first arrived in Jordan, we saw a sign with King Abdullah II's picture and several statements about why Jordan was a great country for business. One of the statements was *rule of law.* My wife and I looked at the traffic and the seemingly obvious disregard for the rules of the road and scoffed at the sign. What I am suggesting in this section is that the rule of law can mean something different in different cultures and still be an accurate statement. *Rule of law* does not have to mean rigid adherence to bureaucratic practice or rules.

In Iraq, I saw many US officers frustrated with what they perceived to be an endless process of negotiations. At no point in the contract process for foreign military sales did the Iraqis cease to negotiate. They were always trying to get a better deal or more concessions. The US officers did not understand that their counterparts did not see the contract as set in stone, but rather as a sand dune that could always be changed.

Nothing is final.

The word no implies finality. When an American says, "No, I do not want to go to dinner," that is a final answer. Arab culture requires that an invitation be offered multiple times, and basic rules of politeness mean that the offer must be refused at least initially, even if the intent is to ultimately accept. If one does not offer multiple times, then one is not serious in one's offer. If one does not refuse multiple times, then one is not sincere in one's refusal. These are basic rules of behavior in Arab culture. This will be addressed again later when discussing hospitality. The point here is that there is no finality except from God. It is one of the reasons why an Arab will rarely tell a guest no when asked for a favor.

Early in my service in Iraq, I sat in a conference where various initiatives were discussed. These were all initiatives proffered by the US side to assist the Iraqi military in their modernization with new equipment and training. The meeting was US and NATO only. In the meeting one of the US civilians present mentioned one initiative that had been offered to the Iraqis almost a year earlier and that had sat on the desk of the minister of defense for that entire time without a response. He recommended that a senior US leader demand a response. I spoke up and said that an answer had been given; the answer was no. By not answering the written proposal, the minister of defense was saying no, without speaking the word. The other gentleman then said that we should force the minister to say the word. I shook my head in dismay and then stated that one does not force an Arab to say no without doing harm to the relationship. It should be enough to understand the cultural reasons for refusing the offer. Additionally, a no implied by inaction is not a final no, but rather a no for the current period. A stated no is a final no, of sorts.

Time in the Middle East is about flow, not linearity. I have previously discussed position versus progress, and time plays a part in this. Just because time passes does not mean things will or should necessarily improve. When the Kuwaitis were pressed on a post-oil production plan, one US diplomat heard the following statement: "My grandfather rode a camel, my father drove a car, I have a Mercedes, and my son may ride a camel." There is a fatalistic sense that time will bring what it brings—see the discussion on will and submission.

My first few weeks in the United Arab Emirates were dominated by the use of one English word: flexibility. I have heard the concept if not the word used repeatedly in other countries throughout the region. It is a plea from the Arabs and the Israelis for the US to be more flexible. US policies and procedures are rigid and inflexible. For a bedouin, inflexibility equals death.

Any person who functions in severe climates knows that it is essential to adjust decisions and plans to the weather and terrain conditions. To move forward without regard for the situation is a certain recipe for disaster. This is also true in nearly all military endeavors. The enemy, the weather, and the terrain all get a vote. Despite the built-in understanding in military culture for the need to be flexible, our policies regarding foreign assistance are anything but flexible, and they impede our ability to work with potential friends and allies.

Where did these policies come from? Were they divinely decreed from above? Did the finger of God carve them into stone? Of course not. This is also true of the standards that the military and businesses use regarding maintenance, training, and systems integration. In most cases Westerners behave as if these are heaven-sent rather than stepping back and objectively assessing the possibility for adjustment, change, or flexibility.

To an Arab nothing is fixed. There is always room for discussion, understanding, and flexibility. Even in the Koran, a *hadith* (a quoted statement from the prophet Mohammed) says that each verse has multiple layers of meaning, with the highest meaning known only to God. Even in the Koran—which is viewed by non-Muslims as the most intransigent part of Arab culture—there is room for greater understanding and a possible change in meaning and interpretation.

During my first road trip from Abu Dhabi to Dubai, I noted a speed limit sign that read 120 kilometers per hour. A few hundred meters further down the highway was a very large sign that explained that the maximum speed allowable was 140. I love those two signs, as they communicate so much about the differences in culture between the West and the Arab world. For Americans, the speed limit is a limit or a line that cannot be crossed without consequence. In the Middle East, most rules like this have flexibility built in: the limit is 120, but you will not be ticketed until you pass the maximum speed of 140. A different perspective.

# Example #10
## Education:
# Memorization vs. Discovery

ducation shapes how people think. Some of the challenges between cultures often stem from the different manners in which people are educated. Over the last several decades the US educational system has increasingly emphasized a system of discovery learning, which focuses on the student taking responsibility for his or her ability to apply the principles taught. The teacher is viewed as a guide, one who points the way forward. Rote memorization is not encouraged, and in some classrooms is belittled and shunned.

The Arab world emphasized mass literacy centuries before Europe and more than a millennium before the United States existed as a country. Literacy prior to mass publication through moveable type was possible through memorization. In the case of Arabs, this meant memorization of Koranic verses. Even today there are competitions similar to spelling bees and geography bees in which children recite as much of the Koran as they can. Every year at least one child is able to recite the Koran in its entirety from memory—more than six thousand verses!

The education system of early Islam has carried over into modern times. Some schools throughout the Arab world still focus on rote memorization of the Koran as the centerpiece of their educational platform. Even in secular schools, the style of education is based on this long tradition of memorization. Such a tradition places the onus on the teacher to provide the material that needs to be learned, memorized, and repeated on the test. If a student fails a test, it is either because he or she failed to memorize everything or the teacher failed to provide the information to be memorized. A test that includes questions with answers not previously discussed for memorization is viewed as a deception and a failure on the part of the teacher.

Differences in educational philosophy come into play when students from one culture enter the classrooms of a different culture. This happens when Arab students come to Western courses of instruction. These students tend to struggle because the questions and answers on the test are not usually discussed in the class itself. Rather the underlying principles are discussed, with the expectation that students understand them sufficiently to apply them to test questions.

Cheating is also viewed differently. As discovery education expects students to apply the knowledge gained, there is little opportunity for collaborative testing—what matters is your application of the principles taught. In a memorization approach, every student has memorized the same material for the same application. Sharing the answers of that memorization is viewed similar to a classmate explaining how to use a calculator during a test. It is the application of the memory tool and not a violation of individual thinking.

Creative processes are not unknown to Arabs. Creativity is simply not a foundational aspect of education.

The dynamic of the student–teacher contract is directly related to this topic. As previously alluded to, in the US the contract goes something like this: the teacher is expected to provide the general rule and examples illustrating how to apply this rule. The student is expected to pay attention and sufficiently learn the rule to be able to apply it in different and non-rehearsed scenarios. For example, mathematics is one area in which both learning styles require memorization, as every student is expected to know and memorize math facts. In the Arab world, the student–teacher contract implies that the teacher must present the material for memorization and the student must memorize the material. From an Arab perspective a teacher who tests on information not presented in class is violating this contract and is setting the student up for failure. When one is set up to fail, then there is no shame in ceasing effort and quitting.

The clash of cultures regarding education is apparent. To an Arab, the US student–teacher contract is almost, by definition, deceptive and defeating. Tests are usually not completely based on material provided in the classroom; ergo, teachers seek to cause students to fail. From a US perspective, Arab students are not critical thinkers. Anyone who has watched Arab students study knows that they are not lazy. They can be amazingly disciplined and tremendously focused. Their focus is on committing the presented material to memory for the test, which requires regurgitation of that same information.

One example of the US model came when we returned to the US after more than eight years of sending our children to international schools in the Middle East. One of our children was in the eighth grade, and in the school open house we listened as our son's literature teacher explained her grading procedures. She said that after each test, she spends a class period going over the tests. Students are allowed to argue for their answers. If they make a solid argument, they can get their points back. She indicated that some students have been able to raise their grade significantly in this manner. She believes there is real value in being able to support a thought process and back it up with facts. She values the ability to reason over memorization of facts.

The difference between these two education models has an effect on how people think and, in particular, the way they solve problems. Americans value problem solving, or the path. Arabs value the end result, or destination. This is a different perspective from that of law and finality. The law is unchanging in the US view, but flexible in the Arab view. Education is unchanging in the Arab view, but flexible in the US view. This can be linked backed to the roots of culture. Arab–Muslims value Islam above all else. You can't argue with what God says; you can only memorize it and try to follow it. Americans have always been about finding new, better ways to do things. We value research and developmental processes and are always looking for new ways to achieve the best results. Clearly our way is not the only way or necessarily the best way, since our test scores do not rank highly on the world scene, but it is a way that supports what we value.

I have seen these problems played out again and again in US military classrooms, where students are required to apply a creative approach to the information presented. Arab officers either quickly conclude that they have been set up to look foolish and withdraw from participation, or just play along with limited effort. US officers tend to struggle when roles are reversed, as they do not have the memorization skills required for high scores.

# Part One Conclusion

We are different! The previous ten examples do not in any way represent a comprehensive list of all the differences between Arabs and Americans. These are some that I see as most significant and have the greatest impact on understanding that we are different. Difference is not bad. The preceding sections should have made it clear that this book was not written to criticize, but to identify. Negative points of American culture were provided to cause one to think critically and understand why one thinks the way one does.

It is always dangerous to point out differences in cultures, as this tends to lead to the ancient Greek use of the label "barbarian" to derogatorily identify those who speak different languages and demonstrate different traits. That said, I take the risk because I have witnessed firsthand the damage that is done when people enter meetings assuming commonalities that do not exist. It is much better to enter a meeting assuming difference and spending more time in communication to clearly state goals, visions, and intent than it is to quickly agree and move forward based on a poor foundation of false mutual agreement.

For those bees who are reading this, I offer the following three key points to consider.

- If one has the desire to inspire the counterpart to DO something, then the conversation must be shaped to make the doing seem logical within the construct of the counterpart.

- What gets a spider to do something is different from what gets a bee to do something. This must be considered prior to the meeting if one truly wants to achieve success.
- Conducting the meeting on a bee-only framework will end in frustration, as the spider will see no value in the logic or arguments.

Too often Americans fail to follow these three simple points. The US military officers I observed (and usually myself as well) conduct meetings as they are comfortable—like bees—and the spiders present do not always or even usually follow along. The meeting ends, heads nod, handshakes are offered, and then no results happen.

Please note that real bees and spiders exist in nearly every climate and can and do thrive together. The fact that two cultures are so different does not mean there must be conflict or even frustration. Once one understands the cultural paradigm of the other, then it is possible for productive dialogue and cooperation to exist.

# Part
# TWO
## Developing Empathy

# ☙ Developing Empathy

The art of influence necessitates developing empathy. The examples of differences in this book are provided to help readers question their own cultural perspective—to allow them to understand how they perceive the pyramid. Then they can develop an understanding of *the other* and how they see the pyramid. Understanding is the simplest part of empathy, involving only data and information. Empathy is about using that understanding to place oneself in the other's perspective and to see the pyramid from their position.

In this discussion of empathy, I will address a concept that I call *walls*. The walls to which I refer are conceptual walls that require great communicative sensitivity to avoid losing an opportunity for influence. Ignoring or failing to address wall issues will result in harm to the relationship rather than its advancement. Some of the wall issues have already been introduced, but here they will be identified as such and discussed in a way that allows the reader to avoid the associated challenges and pitfalls.

This effort to understand and develop empathy is carried out with the intent of developing influence. This is not a manipulation-focused process. I believe that when one develops empathy, one loses much of the selfish motivation. Influence combined with empathy creates a relationship that benefits both sides.

# First Thing

This story takes place in February 1986 far from the Middle East—north of the Arctic Circle. The main character is US Army Captain Michael Ferriter. At that time Captain Ferriter was a company commander of C Company, 6th Battalion, 327th Infantry Regiment. He and his company were conducting a maneuver training exercise with the Alaskan National Guard.

Captain Ferriter parachuted onto the snow-covered plain of northern Alaska. After he landed in the snow and fell over, as he was taught to do, he looked up to see a pair of mukluks next to him. The owner of these large, furry boots was Command Sergeant Major (CSM) Washington[15], a native Eskimo and the battalion CSM of the Alaskan National Guard unit. CSM Washington was a paragon of the Eskimo, as he wore the stereotypical coat with a deep hood and fur trim.

Captain Ferriter pushed himself up from the snow, organized his company, and directed them toward the objective some four kilometers away. The Eskimo battalion fell in as well and conducted their operation in concert. This regular training exercise was successful. At its conclusion the soldiers prepared

---

[15] Interestingly, many Eskimos adopted their current family names based on the names of the presidents of the United States when the trappers or traders came through. CSM Washington had a traditional Eskimo first name but a very English-sounding last name. Many of the other soldiers had last names like Jefferson, Madison, etc. Clearly presidents are powerful men, and to have such a name for your family was considered good.

their sleeping and protection arrangements—in snow caves.

Later in the evening, as they sat in their snow caves and the soldiers were all bedded down, Captain Ferriter sat with CSM Washington and the battalion commander. Curious to understand the native strengths and abilities in this very harsh climate, Captain Ferriter laid out a hypothetical operational scenario for the CSM. He asked the CSM how he would conduct the operation, which involved attacking a distant objective, maybe twenty kilometers away, in bad weather and over difficult terrain. The specifics of the tactical scenario are unimportant—what is of value was the CSM's answer.

The CSM answered, "The first thing is to survive."

This seemed an odd answer and only vaguely related to the tactical scenario outlined. Of course one needs to survive. Captain Ferriter nodded and said, "Yeah, got that. But do you send a scouting party forward and have the rest bring up the heavy gear later, or what? How do you deal with the problem?"

The CSM answered, "The first thing is to survive."

Now it seemed like the CSM was truly failing to recognize the importance of the mission and the need to complete the task assigned. Captain Ferriter posed his questions in several different ways, trying to pry from this short-spoken native the secrets of his people in operating in the harsh climate. No matter how many times or in how many ways Captain Ferriter posed the question, the CSM never came off the importance of surviving.

It became clear that in the harsh and extremely demanding environment of the Arctic Circle, survival was and is the preeminent consideration—all other aspects pale in comparison.

Years later, Lieutenant General Michael Ferriter explained this story to me after meeting with Iraqi officials. He was seeking to relay the importance of survival among cultures steeped in the harshest environments. He explained that many of those who had negotiated with the Iraqi Prime Minister or other senior leaders seemed to think that the issues and concerns of their Iraqi counterparts were political or economic, and that if they could figure out the right angle or the right incentive, then the Iraqi official would change his mind and adopt the American perspective and desired behavior. This was probably not the right way, he explained to me, as the Iraqi leaders were products of a culture formed in the harsh deserts; in most cases they were concerned with the challenge of survival and would not move beyond CSM Washington's "first thing."

I believe that if I were to make a certain offer to a classroom full of American students, they might accept it.[16] The offer would be that if the student were able to successfully travel one hundred miles across a desert without any additional water, I would give them one thousand dollars. At this relatively low amount, there may be one or more takers. But if the monetary reward continued to increase, I believe that at some point nearly every student would take the offer. I have discussed a scenario similar to this with bedouin, though the specifics were different. My experience is that no amount of money would entice most bedouin to attempt such a challenge. Why? What is the difference? The bedouin knows that the challenge will result in death. No amount of money will change the result; death for one thousand or death for one billion is still death. They understand the first thing: survive. A young American typically does not. They tend to believe that given enough enticement, anything is possible. It is an aspect of the American dream. If you work hard enough, if you want something badly enough, you can make it happen. Americans typically call this optimism.

---

[16] I have tested this theory on numerous occasions and there is a monetary value at which most US students will accept the challenge. There are always a few students who share the bedouin realization of danger.

But in the case of the bedouin—and the Arab in general—
you can cajole all you want, but a bedouin is not going to leave
a secure and safe position to journey without water across the
desert. He will never do it, no matter how important the mission,
because what good is the mission if you are dead in the middle
of the desert? Their entire behavior is built around the notion of
CSM Washington's first thing—survive.

I will go back to the spider analogy. Imagine the spider on
his web. On that web is a safe area. For some spiders that area
may be quite small, and for other spiders that area is much larger,
maybe encompassing the entire web. In either case the spider
will typically stay within the safe area of the web, fighting to
maintain an element of security. Regardless of the relative size
of the safe area, all spiders are constrained to operate within
their web. From the perspective of a bee this may seem odd, as
bees are not constrained to a location. Though one can argue the
relative security of the two metaphors, the important point is
that a bee may see a spider's emphasis on maintaining position
as odd.

As we begin a discussion on understanding, it is critical to
understand this about your counterparts: what is their perception
of security? Where are they safe? Can they risk making dramatic
changes, or must they be extremely conservative?

I observed the actions and decisions of the Iraqi prime
minister in 2010–2011. The more I came to understand this
principle and the political realities in Iraq, the more I started
to understand that he was making his decisions with the intent
to stay well inside his safe area. My observation is that he
believed he could only move across a small portion of his web
without risking his position. Most of his actions with regard to
the security services and the parliament were designed to both
expand his safe area and avoid undue risk. I believe that the

failure to secure a larger and longer US presence in Iraq post-2011 was a direct result of US officials not understanding this simple and foundational aspect of the prime minister's behavior. They did not recognize that the Iraqi Prime Minister was living according to the same rule espoused by CSM Washington—the first thing is to survive.

# Understanding "The Other"

*I don't like that man. I must get to know him better.*

—Abraham Lincoln

Understanding is a prerequisite for empathy. Without it, reaching our goal of influence is impossible. The good news is that understanding is the easiest part in the process that moves from understanding to empathy to influence. Most classes on culture focus solely on understanding or a portion of understanding. This is Culture 101. The methods for achieving understanding that I will suggest here do not include a list of do's and don'ts, though I do recommend some things to do and some things to avoid doing. These methods are about developing a more comprehensive concept of understanding.

An example of understanding that led to real influence in the Arab world involves the British officer John Baggot Glubb. Here was a man who served in the Arab world for thirty-six years (from 1920–1956). He commanded Arab units in training and combat and was tasked with the development of an Arab army in the British protectorate of Transjordan. He spoke, read, and wrote Arabic and had a masterful understanding of the nuances of the culture and language. After his service for the Hashemite Kingdom of Jordan ended, he went on to write several excellent books on Arab and Islamic history. He is one of the best examples of an expert that I can suggest. He truly *understood.*

Of course he did! He spent thirty-six years developing this understanding. How many companies, businesses, or government entities will invest thirty-six years in an employee to help him or her get to this level? In my opinion, few to none. I am not suggesting this level of understanding in what follows. The idea is to think through what a person can reasonably do and achieve, and how dedicating a few minutes to an hour a day could make a real difference. Understanding a foreign culture requires a commitment of time. This is not a get-thin-quick diet. However, like dieting, a daily commitment can make a significant difference.

Okay, we are committed to understanding. What do we need to understand? Here are the basic four topics we must study to understand any culture, especially those in the Middle East.
1. Religion
2. History
3. Culture
4. Language

Now to briefly describe each of the four and their importance in contributing to understanding.

### Religion

In the United States and Europe, some circles view devout practitioners of religion as quaint, or even as foolish and backward. Within academia and government service, religion may be viewed as an inconvenience and distraction from the real mission and tasks at hand. Those who believe in such a way often demonstrate difficulty in developing empathy with those for whom religion is a fundamental influence in their life. If you, the reader, are not devoutly religious, then you may need greater imagination to understand one who genuinely is, but I believe it is still possible and very necessary. Not all cultures are devoutly religious, and if you are trying to understand one of the cultures that are not, then no worries.

Religion plays a central role in nearly all Middle Eastern cultures. Even those who claim to be secular are shaped in some ways by the religious practices of the society in which they live. This is true in Christian, Jewish, and Muslim communities, though I will mostly focus on Islam.

For Muslims, the religion of Islam is their entire life. No aspect of their lives is unaffected by their religion. It affects when they wake up. What they wear. What they say when they enter the room. What they eat. What they read. Every aspect of life. This is by no means onerous for the faithful. It is so by design. Islam is not a religion that asks its followers to simply go one day a week to a building and worship and then go home and continue on with a different life. It was always intended as a complete and holistic lifestyle. It is.

To understand Arabic culture in the world today, one must understand Islam. This understanding does not need to include a deep acceptance or immersion in religious doctrine. However, it is extremely useful to grasp the totality and holistic nature of the faith on the lives of the faithful so that one can see, recognize, filter, and understand various actions and attributes and behaviors through the lens of religion.

I will give one example. Early on in my service in the Jordanian Army I sat in a battalion command and staff meeting. One of the officers arrived about twenty-five minutes late for the meeting. In the US military he would have quietly moved into the room and taken his seat without any introduction or attempt to draw attention to himself. In contrast, this Jordanian officer entered the room and in a slightly loud voice stated *salaam aleykum.*[17] He was responded to by the battalion commander and several other officers. I was flabbergasted. Later I understood the requirement for devout Muslims to offer this greeting upon entering any room to extend the peace of God upon all who are in the room. That requirement extends over all rooms at all times and situations. This is a simple way that religion affects the mundane and common aspects of life in a business or normal work environment.

Those who do not take the time to learn these little ways in which religion influences their counterparts will struggle to understand the reasons behind many behaviors, actions, and reactions. I have personally observed challenges arise as American officers interacted with Iraqi and other Muslim counterparts. There have been frustrations over prayer times, holiday observances, and meeting interruptions. In most of these cases, a few minutes of explanation and understanding could have mitigated these challenges.

As I previously stated, I am not giving a lesson on Islam. I definitely do not have the expertise to do so, and there is not sufficient space in this book to address the depth and richness of such a large and dynamic religion. One does not need to become a religious scholar to understand the important aspects of the religion, but one does need to be a lifelong learner and an observer and asker of questions. I have yet to find a Muslim who will not take the time to explain the religious reason for why they do a certain thing. Asking why is usually a good way to develop and deepen a relationship.

### History

During my service in Jordan I was driving through the Yarmouk River valley with my Jordanian battalion commander.

---

[17]This phrase means "peace be upon you." In a more profound way, it means the peace be upon you, or that peace that comes only from God.

As we approached a hill in the valley he pointed and identified the hill as Tel Khalid. He explained that this hill was named for Khalid bin Walid, the great Muslim commander who led the armies of Islam in battles against fellow Arabs, Persians, and Romans. In Yarmouk he participated in a battle against the Roman Empire that changed the trajectory of the region from Christianity to Islam. The battle produced so much blood that as Khalid sat on his horse on the hill, the blood reached the tops of his boots. After relating this to me, my commander turned and looked at me, shrugged, and said, "That may not be completely true." I was somewhat staggered that he could not see the hyperbole in what he recounted. The hilltop is fifty to sixty feet above the valley floor, and the valley itself is several hundred feet wide. I thought there could not be enough blood in the world to fill that valley deep enough to reach the top of a man's boots while sitting on a horse on the hilltop. This experience was extremely important for me to understand my commander's perspective of history.

Islamic history is recorded such that the footnotes, if you will, are given at the beginning of every account. Each paragraph begins with a list of sources that tie the person who recounted the story to the author back through a chain of individuals to a companion of the prophet or the prophet himself. As each person in the chain is considered reliable, the information, by association, is considered reliable. Thus there is little questioning of what is said regardless of what modern scholarship may reveal about the likelihood of numbers of participants in a given battle or the amount of blood flowing through a given valley. As with most Americans, most Muslims are not historians. They do not do their own personal research on topics. Unlike most Americans, most Muslims are conversant in the history they are taught, as this history forms part of the narrative of religious, political, and social issues.

I have too often heard Westerners discount Islamic history or their Muslim associates' understanding of history as superstition or folklore rather than something of real validity. What a mistake!

There are two kinds of history important to understand in this category of understanding—"real history" and their history. The reason I have "real history" in quotes is because I am a historian and I understand that there is no such thing as objective or true history. History has always been a literary form. Each representation of history is told from a particular point of view and using certain selected sources. What people choose as their sources for history shows a great deal about what they value and how they think. It is not sufficient to simply understand the "real history" found online or in history books published by Western companies. At times their history, meaning the history related by average people, tells you more useful information about them.

When I was an instructor at the US Army Armor School, I instructed my student officers to research, write, and present a battle analysis from a list of preselected battles. One of the battles was the Battle of Abu Agheila from the 1956 Arab–Israeli War. In this particular battle the Israelis attacked the Egyptians in the Sinai Peninsula. In this class of about eighty officers there were nine international officers, five of whom were Egyptian. The international officers were not required to attend the presentations, and normally only one or two did. On this occasion all the Egyptian and other Arab officers were there. At the end of the presentation one of the four presenters asked if there were any questions or comments. Four of the five Egyptian officers raised their hands. Once acknowledged, they began to pepper the US officers with questions about sources and perspective. Specifically they asked if the sources were Israeli. They challenged the accuracy of the presentation, explaining that the quoted number of Egyptian forces in the defensive position was wrong and the overall context of the battle was inaccurately portrayed. The US officers defended their academic honor and integrity against the offended national pride and dignity of the Egyptian military. I sat back for several minutes to watch and learn. It was a great experience to hear the other side of such a discussion. I could see that much of the US source material was derived or taken directly from Israeli material and only a little was from the Egyptian perspective. I eventually called a halt, as tempers started to rise on both sides. I thanked everyone and went to talk to the US presenters. They were angry. I tried to explain to them the once-in-a-lifetime experience they had just had. I did not explain it well, as few of the tempers were calmed to everyone's satisfaction.

Several years later I had the opportunity to visit the fortifications of the Bar Lev line. These were Israeli-constructed defensive positions along the eastern bank of the Suez Canal. These were the forts taken in the early hours of the Egyptian assault across the canal in October 1973. During this visit I was able to hear the Egyptian interpretation of the Israeli defenses and fortifications. Later I visited the 1973 War memorial in Cairo and another in Damascus. I was also able to visit numerous Israeli memorials and historical interpretive sites. From these experiences I learned how different the historical presentations were on each side of the fighting—different to the point of representing almost completely different engagements and battles. I now could reflect on the emotional response of my Egyptian officer students and appreciate their anger at what they saw as misrepresented truth.

The internet clearly empowers our learning. It is a relatively simple feat to study just one small historical event each day or week. It is also much easier to read interpretations from multiple perspectives. As one studies such history, real benefit comes from eliciting a historical discussion with one's counterpart and then listening to the history from the counterpart's point of view. This is how the counterpart sees and understands the history.

### Culture

There are many definitions of culture, but here I want to use a simple definition: how people act and interact. Later I will give my thoughts on the great aspects of Arab culture, but here I simply want to express the importance of understanding culture to understand a person. Why a person acts in a particular way profoundly shapes how that person thinks, sees the world, and sees themselves in the world. This includes an appreciation of familial relationships, the treatment of guests, the behavior and expectations of the host, and the interaction of the genders, not to mention many other things. Of the four things discussed in understanding people, this is probably the area that organizations spend the most time on. I would challenge that the value of such instruction is limited to the depth sought in the instruction and discussion. Simply conducting discussions on a Culture 101 level will not provide what I am suggesting. It is necessary to go beyond actions and interactions to the motivations, reasons, and whys of the observable. That is when understanding can be derived from simple data.

My family and I had only been in Jordan for a few days when we were invited to celebrate Eid al-Adha with the family of one of my former students. Our hosts were my student's father and mother. The father had previously served in the United States. They were understanding of our newness to Arab culture, and they were patient with my halting and problematic Arabic. We all—men and women—sat in one room. The mother and sister of my student were engaging and used to Americans. In many ways this was a very friendly and easy way to break into the new culture.

The traditional dinner for Eid al-Adha in Jordan is the national dish, mensaf. The holiday itself can be translated as "the feast of the slaughter," and it is the celebration at the end of Ramadan that commemorates the angel who stopped Abraham from offering his son as a sacrifice. Therefore the primary food is lamb or goat. While we sat in our host's home we were treated to an explanation of the story of Abraham and the command to sacrifice his son Ishmael. When I heard Ishmael's name I thought that our host had made a mistake, as in Christianity and Judaism the belief is that Abraham was asked to sacrifice Isaac. I did not mention anything about the "mistake," as I thought it was simply a slip of the tongue. When he said Ishmael the second time, my wife spoke up and said, "I think you mean Isaac." Our host smiled kindly and said somewhat condescendingly, "We call him Ishmael." My eyes opened a little wider as I realized that here was part of the root difference, the very foundations of the religion divergence: Isaac (Jewish or Christian) and Ishmael (Muslim).

*Mensaf* is a dish whose name is derived from the Arabic word for explosion. It is served on a large platter covered in rice and pine nuts. Bits of cooked lamb or goat are placed on the platter as if they had exploded from the center, where sits the head of the slaughtered animal. A hot yoghurt sauce is then poured over the meat and rice. My youngest son was four years old at this time, and he stared at the animal head as he approached the table and kept his eyes fixed on the head throughout the meal.

The meal is usually served by the host. In Arab culture it is important that guests be satisfied, so the host will give them large portions and continue to add food to their plates until they are almost physically restrained. One does not clear one's plate in Arab culture. Doing so communicates that one has not received enough. A good host keeps the food coming at such a pace that it is nearly impossible to clear one's plate even if one is so inclined.

While in Jordan I read an article written by a newspaper columnist about the cultural meaning of *mensaf.* This dish communicates the Jordanian bedouin culture. It is served on a single platter from which all members of the assembled group eat. This makes it easier for a bedouin tribe to carry and clean it. The meal is made from rice, which is light to carry and easy to cook; sheep or goats that move with the family; and yoghurt sauce made by reconstituting a yoghurt ball that has been dried to preserve the flavor and extend shelf life, so to speak.

This one meal was a great example of how understanding culture can lead to understanding a person and his or her foundational beliefs and behaviors. For me and my family, this dinner was our true introduction to Arab culture and experience.

I want to close this section with my most important comments about culture. However one defines culture, one should keep in mind that culture is what defines a person and people. I have often heard business, government, and military people say, "I get the culture part . . . ," as if culture is simply an outer garment that a person puts on as he or she prepares to walk out the door. Culture is not a uniform, a coat, a shawl, a handbag, or any other accoutrement that one throws on or grabs for such and such occasion. It is the core aspect of a human's nature—it is one's being and self-definition.

However one grasps the concepts in this book or any other regarding cross-cultural interaction, I ask that one does not make the mistake of dealing with the cultural aspects and implications of an engagement as if it were simply something to get through so that the real work can be done. Every engagement conducted on this basis has little lasting value. It is cursory and utilitarian only. I expect the counterpart will only deal with you as they have to and tolerate your cursory and superficial attempts. Too often I have heard Arabs share with me their thoughts on those who do not understand them or their culture. Typically they are referring to persons from the US, though I have heard similar comments about those from a great many other countries. I believe that in most cases, the non-Arab person to whom they referred thought they had made a valiant effort at cultural sensitivity and awareness. In many ways such people are viewed as I would be if I were to attend fashion week somewhere—I may know the name of a designer, but I have no understanding of the industry or the significance of any given design or designer. I would be going through the motions, and that is true of many who interact in the Arab world.

## Language

The German philosopher Ludwig Wittgenstein said, "The limits of my language means the limits of my world." When understanding the other, language is profound. The language of your opponent or counterpart tells a great deal about them. There is much to say about Arabic in comparison to English. Too much for this book. I will make a few short notes to serve the overall purpose of developing understanding.

The fact that English is read from left to right and Arabic from right to left is a great example of the differences in language. Earlier in this book I identified the explicit versus implicit natures of the two languages and also the direct versus poetic aspects. As this book seeks to be more than simply about Americans understanding Arabs, I want to identify a framework for using languages to understand different cultures generally and Arabic culture specifically.

Much of a conversation in Arabic is made up of greeting.

There are a lot of different ways to ask "how are you?" As this exchange of questions (rarely with detailed answers) occurs at the beginning of nearly all interactions, this is the first part of the Arabic language I would recommend a person learn. Learn how to ask how someone is, how their family is, and if they have any news. Also learn appropriate responses for each.

It is of benefit to understand the nuances and subdivisions within each Arab country and how they speak to each other. Many Jordanian Christians explained that Arab Christians do not greet each other with *salaam aleykum,* which they view as an exclusively Muslim phrase. The Arab Christians there greet each other with the less religiously charged *marhaba.* When I shared this with Arab Christian coworkers from Iraq, they were shocked by such an attitude and shared with me that Christ entered homes with the phrase *peace be unto you,* or in Arabic *salaam aleykum,* and therefore such a phrase is not Muslim, Jewish, or Christian. It is a phrase for all religions.

I personally find such an interpretation enlightened. Though something may be the case in Iraq, it may not be true in Jordan or in other places either. For this reason I recommend gathering information on nuances within the specific culture in which you interact before making an assumption on the proper way to greet.

Arabic is the language of God to Muslims and is therefore the language of Islam. It is very useful to keep this in mind. I shared earlier the experience of a Jordanian officer entering a staff meeting late and greeting the room with *salaam aleykum.* He did so because this is an expectation of Muslims—as a faithful Muslim enters a room he or she is to greet those within with this invocation. There are other directive aspects of speech, naming, and other uses of the language that come from the Koran, the *hadith,* or the *sunna.*

Another recommendation is to use a simple understanding

of the language to your benefit. My first name is Brian, and for whatever reason it is a difficult name for many Arabic speakers to remember. Often it gets confused with Ibrahim, the Arabic version of Abraham. Even native English speakers often forget my last name, and the number of times I have been called Steve is without count. I have learned to use my Arabic *kunya* instead. A *kunya* is the "father of" or "mother of" name—in Arabic, *Abu* or *Um,* respectively. My oldest son is named Hunter, and therefore in Arabic I am the father of Hunter, or *Abu Sayad.* No Arab names their son Hunter, so this name is unusual and therefore memorable. On occasion I have also used this as the source of a joke. I follow my *kunya* with the line, "This is my terrorist name."[18] The idea that a US Army officer would have a terrorist name is always funny, and it gets remembered even more. Many times I am now greeted as *Abu Sayad,* and that is how I am known.

I knew a US advisor to an Iraqi officer who also used his *kunya* to great effect in his relationship with the Iraqi soldiers. His oldest son is Joseph. All names from the Bible are already translated into Arabic, and many of them are used in Arabic families as well. Thus he became *Abu Yousef* and wore a stitched nametag saying such on his left shoulder. Iraqi soldiers stopping him at various checkpoints would see that nametag in Arabic and smile and warmly pass him through. He may not have been one of them, but he was considered to be one who *got it.*

I have seen over and over again how much benefit of the doubt is given to one who gets it or one who demonstrates that they are making an honest effort. Almost everywhere I have been, with one notable exception, Arabs have loved the fact that I try to speak in Arabic.

---

[18] Most terrorists take a nom de guerre and do not regularly use their real name. My joke plays on understanding this trait. Humor can cut both ways, and thus one needs to be somewhat comfortable in the language and culture before one tries to introduce themselves as having a "terrorist name."

Whenever I have given the presentations from which this book is derived, every native Arab speaker and ethnic Arab in the audience has greatly enjoyed the presentation. They may disagree with some detail—Iraqis are not Jordanians, or that is based on bedouin culture more than Egyptian, et cetera—but they universally appreciate the purpose of the presentation and this book: to understand them and their people, however broadly or narrowly defined, on their own terms and not from a Western perspective.

If you make the effort, the relationship will develop in a positive fashion. That is the single biggest point here.

Understanding the language is critical to understanding the people who speak it. I know how hard Arabic is to learn. I am not as fluent as I would like, and I sometimes struggle to get my point across. Speaking a foreign language risks a great deal, as simple grammatical errors make one look dumb. My above points should give one a good reason to risk it and accept looking dumb and foolish to help the relationship grow.

LTG Michael Ferriter, for whom I worked in Iraq, always carried around Arabic flash cards. As we drove to meetings he would rehearse words and phrases that he might want to use to emphasize a particular point or to simply engage more effectively with his counterpart. He also used these cards as a way to break down relationship barriers by asking his Iraqi counterparts to quiz him. This may not have changed hardened positions. It did create a friendly and positive atmosphere, and it clearly communicated his willingness to make an effort. I believe it did help him in his engagements.

### The Pyramid

Remember the earlier reference to the pyramid. Understanding is about seeing the pyramid from their perspective. What do they see when they look at this shape? One may not get all the way over to the perspective of one's counterpart, but it is possible to get much closer than is currently the case. The effort to understand religion, *their* history, *real* history, culture, and language will assist in both one's own actual understanding and the relationship between counterparts.

This is not as hard and daunting as it sounds. With the technological aids and materials available today, so much can be done in fifteen to thirty minutes a day. I do not say this to sound like an infomercial. A short and consistent commitment can yield great results.

Those responsible for larger organizations may have the influence to invest resources in training people more thoroughly in these aspects. Just because some insight can be gained with little time and effort, it should not prevent those who have the luxury from investing greater time and effort to attain real subject matter specialization. This is an area where the payoff is much greater than the commitment.

# Why the US Is Hated on the Arab Street

I have ridden in many cabs in the Middle East and each time I have learned something about the region and the perceptions of its people. Numerous television shows and movies include the wisdom of a cab driver, and I have come to generally accept that as true to life. They certainly know their lives and have a good sense of their larger community. If one wants to get into a good political discussion, I recommend taking a cab. Many cab drivers have shared with me their frustrations over US policy. They would go to great lengths to express that disagreement with US policy did not equal anger toward or dislike of Americans. Usually the driver would either state or indicate that he (they have all been men) liked and maybe even respected the opportunities available in the US. They would like to go there and cash in.

I have not yet made my points about the strengths and positive aspects of Arab culture. Here is one I will elaborate on later and have commented on previously as well. Arabs value hospitality, and it is a defining characteristic of the culture at large. As a result, Arabs are reluctant to personally criticize anyone even remotely considered a guest. Given this aspect of Arab personality, any criticism of a person's connections should stand out in stark relief.

In *Piercing the Fog of War,* I wrote a chapter as a case study for developing empathy, and that case study was on what drives an individual to become a suicide terrorist. I will not rewrite that chapter here, but much of what I will say here can be compared and contrasted with those notes. Here I want to focus simply on the anger and what motivates it. I expect this will be a sensitive issue, and I want to move forward with a brief experience I had late in 2011.

I was working on writing another project, and I received some recommendations to add some statistical information from public polling to my work. I began internet research and came across a Zogby polling site. James Zogby is an American citizen of Arab ethnic origin and the founder of the Arab American Institute. His organization, among other things, conducts surveys and polls in the Middle East, and the information from these surveys and polls provides some of the best statistical insights into the Arab world and its view of the US.[19] Though I did not have a rosy picture of how Arabs saw the US, the information I found painted a gloomier picture than I expected. I followed this polling information with some direct questions to an Arab military[20] officer with whom I was working closely for a week. I asked him for his perspective on how the US was viewed within his country. He said that most of his countrymen did not like the US, and many hated our policies. Once again, not surprising. It was enlightening, as the general perception of the Americans working in this same country was that we were all loved. In fact,

---

[19] For more information, I direct readers to the Arab American Institute for their own research (http://www.aaiusa.org/pages/opinion-polls/). The specific poll referenced in this chapter is titled "Arab Attitude, 2011" and is available for download at http://www.aaiusa.org/reports/arab-attitudes-2011.

[20] I am excluding the name of the country to avoid unintended embarrassment. The point here is not to single out a specific country, but to make clear that Americans and the policies of our country are not well loved in the region as a whole. This single experience is indicative of numerous other experiences I had over more than eight years of traveling in the Middle East and North Africa.

when I was relating this information to another US officer in the presence of a member of the US embassy staff, the response of the embassy staff member was that she had never heard or suspected that we (Americans) were not liked or that our presence was not appreciated. Why? I believe that the reason for such an attitude is that which was stated above—a good host does not insult a guest regardless of how odious or annoying the guest might be.

They dont like us," and we have no idea.

To understand this dislike of US policies, one thing must be kept in mind: the relationship between the US and Israel. In the Middle East, the US is perceived to be directly linked to Israel. Any action taken by Israel is seen as action taken by the US or, at the very least, as action taken after consultation with the US. This may not seem reasonable to many Americans, but ask any cab driver in the Muslim world and I expect this point will be supported. As much as people want to brush this point aside, one does so at one's peril when trying to understand the Arab and Middle Eastern populations.

I have heard visiting US military officers simply state that if this is how the Arabs feel, they need to "get over it" and "move beyond it." I have also heard from experienced US officers something to the effect that if the Arabs feel this way, then why don't they unite and defeat Israel, as the entire united power of the Arab world would be overwhelming.

This is not a book about Middle Eastern politics, so I will not go further down this road. I believe that those who make the above statements do not understand Arabs very well or understand the dynamics of the Middle East. It is possible for the people to have passionate feelings on an issue that the government does not represent in its global position or international policy. This is true of most countries. Such behavior should not be used as an argument that the passions of the people are incorrectly conveyed or understood.

## *Humiliation*

What I want to emphasize in the rest of this section is the power of humiliation. There is and has been for more than a generation (in some cases this has lasted for several hundred years) a deep sense of humiliation on the Arab street. The fact that Arab people have had foreign overlords for centuries has served to generate much of this feeling. Some of this goes back to the Mongol invasions of the fourteenth century and then the Turkish leadership and domination of the region and Islam from the fifteenth and sixteenth centuries until World War I. The conquest of the Muslim world by Europe in the 1800s and 1900s served to make this problem worse in that the overlord was no longer a foreign Muslim, but a foreign non-Muslim. The existence and continued military success of the Jewish state of Israel has been one of the greatest sources of humiliation. Jews were formerly considered a protected people within Islam—meaning a people who did not have the right to bear arms and were to be watched over by Muslims. Now Jews are the militarily dominant people in the region.

When strong Arab leaders have risen up, they have been crushed by the West or the West has sought to crush them. This is true of Gamal Abdel Nasser, Saddam Hussein, Yasser Arafat, Hafez al-Assad, et cetera Many Arabs do not like these men and do not respect how they led or what they did, but these men and others are recognized for being strong and independent personalities who were isolated and attacked verbally, politically, and sometimes militarily by Western powers.

Humiliation is a powerful motivation for behavior. Adolph Hitler used the post-World War I humiliation of the German people as a means to generate the popular support to rise to power. Riots in a variety of places and times have been fueled by the greater sense of humiliation of the people. The events of

2011, commonly referred to as the Arab Spring, show what the humiliated masses can do when a spark ignites the fuel to flame. The full outcome of this movement is yet to be known. One can hope that it will result in greater freedom, opportunity, and benefits for the people who live in the Middle East and North Africa. It is certain that it has not fully played out and much of the story has yet to be written.

In 2012, a film clip supposedly from a movie about the prophet Mohammed was uploaded on YouTube. The video clip was insulting of the prophet. Reaction to the video clip was intense in various parts of the Muslim and Arab world. Insulting the prophet is considered a crime in many places in the Middle East and is a humiliating attack on the honor of all Muslims. During this period of protests and strong reactions, I was asked why the reactions were so intense. Why do Arabs act out so extremely from apparently small offenses? Think on some of the offenses that have had strong reactions from 2005–2012 or so. A few include cartoons of the prophet Mohammed published in a Danish newspaper, a US military person using the Koran for target practice, US military personnel improperly disposing of and burning Korans, a US minister threatening to burn Korans and then doing so, and publication of intentionally offensive satirical comics and films about Islam and the prophet Mohammed. This short list is by no means inclusive. In most cases these represent very small acts conducted by one person or a small group of people in relatively obscure publications or locations. Yet the reactions have included destruction of personal and government property, assaults on people, and death threats against those involved. The reactions seem vastly out of proportion to the generating event. Why?

First, it is worth noting the importance of both the prophet Mohammed and the Koran within Islam and among Muslims.

The Koran is not simply a book. It is not even a book of God. It is *The Word of God*, the unaltered and direct communication of God's word and will to mankind. For those familiar with the beginning of the Gospel of Saint John in the Christian New Testament, the writer refers to Jesus Christ as "The Word."[21] In a very similar sense, the Koran is The Word. Imagine how a Christian would respond to the burning of the person of Jesus Christ—people have been slandered, atrocities performed, and people killed simply over the memory of the crucifixion of Jesus Christ. This is analogous to how many Muslims view the desecration of the Koran. Mohammed's position is that of the greatest of all the prophets. He is also the final prophet who brought the complete and necessary word of God to men. His name is never stated by Muslims without an immediate prayer being offered for God's blessing to be upon him. In many places his name as denoting his person[22] is not written, as he is typically referred to by his title of Prophet.

As one reflects on the seemingly simple events that have attacked the respected symbols of Islam, maybe one is still confused by the intensity of the reaction. To explain this I want to give a simple analogy to communicate the rawness of emotions in this region. Though this overly simplified image may seem a little crass, it conveys my understanding of why the effect is so strong in relation to the perceived cause.

Imagine someone wearing a swimsuit and walking along the

[21] The reference is John 1:1-2, 14, where it is stated "In the beginning was the Word, and the Word was with God, and the Word was God. The same was in the beginning with God. And the Word was made flesh, and dwelt among us, (and we beheld his glory, the glory as of the only begotten of the Father,) full of grace and truth." (King James Translation)

[22] Many Muslim men are named Mohammed, and thus their names are not similarly treated. The name is not held in this universal respect. The respect belongs to the person and his actions.

beach. Another person comes up and dumps a small amount of sand down the swimsuit. Initially this prank may be accepted with some humor or minor annoyance depending on personality and circumstances. The person continues walking along the beach, trying to shake the sand out of the swimsuit. After some time the remaining grains of sand begin to chafe. Now another person comes up and puts a small amount of sand in the swimsuit. This is no longer responded to with humor, but with annoyance. As the person continues to walk, the chafing intensifies and the skin becomes raw and abraded. As this goes on for hours, it leads to bleeding and intense sensitivity. Nothing is now a joke or a prank. Everything, every grain of sand, scrapes and chafes. If the prankster were to attempt to place sand in the swimsuit at this point, they may be greeted with violence and certainly with great annoyance and probably anger.

Events in the Middle East are not single events. No offense against Islam is taken independent of the course of history. One needs to see Arabs as those who have been forced to walk with this sand for years. Their emotions are raw, chafed, and abraded. Another offensive event is greeted in the same way as the prankster who tries to put more sand in the swimsuit. The amount or size of the offense is irrelevant. A pinch, a teaspoon, or a bucket full is still going to inflame the already existing irritation.[23]

Some may want to argue with this analogy. My point is not to justify, but rather to help one to understand and to have empathy. This visualization has helped me to better understand

---

[23] It is critical to understand that I am not trying to justify actions, but to present the perspective of the other. One does not have to agree with their perspective to understand or empathize, but one does need to see it from their side. It should be noted that the lashing out is not simply disproportionate to the offense, by Western standards, but is usually directed against someone who is not associated with the offender—an innocent, if one will allow. This often does not matter to the raw and highly sensitive person who is lashing out.

why Muslims respond so strongly to apparently small offenses.

More will be said on the issue of the US relationship with the Arab people later in the book. The key point to take away here is that the relationships that count in the world of the early twenty-first century are the relationships with the people. In this realm the US reputation is tainted and battered. One cannot merely court the good opinion of the ruling elites and hope to maintain positive relationships for long periods of time.

# Lawrence of Arabia

I am surprised by how many American people I meet who live in the Middle East and have not watched the movie *Lawrence of Arabia*. It is an excellent cinematic accomplishment and a good movie. One might argue that the sweeping camerawork causes the movie to drag at times, and though that might be true, those sweeping images give a sense of bedouin patience and the tendency in the culture to take things in and absorb what is seen. I find the movie instructive of Arab culture in many ways. A particular scene from the movie is especially illustrative of the key points I want to make.

The scene is about forty or so minutes into the film.[24] In this scene the key characters are all seated in the tent of Prince Feisal of Mecca. The others in the tent are Colonel Brighton, T.E. Lawrence (a lieutenant as of this scene), an old man reading the Koran, and later a character called Sherif Ali.

This scene begins with a Koranic recitation by the old man. To see this scene in its cultural context, one needs to imagine it as taking place several hours into the evening. It is probably after midnight, and the colonel is getting sore and tired from listening to the reading in an awkward sitting position. It is also useful to hear this scene as if everyone in it, except Colonel Brighton or those directing comments at Colonel Brighton, is

[24] More specifically, this scene begins at minute 43:49.

speaking Arabic. This helps one to see Colonel Brighton in a more compassionate light. It also places the scene in a much more likely context.

This scene contains many echoes of what one hears in similar engagements throughout the Middle East between American and Arab officers. I will address some of these points in a moment, as this scene also features a variety of great actions and dialogue that are instructive to cultural awareness.

Since I want everyone to watch this movie, I will describe the scene only in brief. The scene begins with the old man reading from the Koran. Prince Feisal completes the reading, and then Lawrence continues the quote. Colonel Brighton asks for a decision on moving from their current position back toward Yenbo and then promises training. Prince Feisal and Sharif Ali want artillery. Lawrence offers a different interpretation of events as he suggests that the bedouin fight in their unique fashion. The scene concludes with a personal conversation between Lawrence and Prince Feisal.

The following are some things to watch for and listen to when viewing this scene. Also following are some of the common themes addressed in the scene that should sound very familiar to so many who have sought to engage Arab military officers. Some of these points will be identified in the pages to follow, and were previously mentioned in the ten examples of differences between bees and spiders.

### Cultural Engagement
- Watch how Colonel Brighton sits and where he faces his feet. Many criticize this behavior, but before one criticizes one should imagine sitting for hours in an uncomfortable position and then think about the best way to adjust without being offensive.

- Lawrence speaks Arabic (please remember the previous comment indicating that this is how the scene would play best in context).
- Lawrence is able to quote the Koran. Immediate credibility!
- Lawrence will later use a Koranic passage to support his argument.
- Use of disagreement to build a relationship. Lawrence disagrees with his superior and says so. He risks the pride of a superior officer to follow the higher purpose of the British objectives.

### Common Themes
- Western emphasis on training
- Arab emphasis on having the latest technology
- Arab belief in the natural fighting prowess of the bedouin or desert warrior
- Distrust of intentions

I am aware that this is an odd way to write a specific example. I strongly recommend that readers of this book watch the scene. While watching it, please keep in mind the ideas discussed here and consider whether the scene can help lead to an understanding of how to excel in a different culture.

I am aware of the criticism and mythology surrounding T.E. Lawrence. Regardless of the hype and hyperbole, many lessons of his story are of tremendous value. For instance, time was irrelevant to effectiveness. Lawrence was able to turn his understanding to empathy and his empathy to influence within days, weeks, and months. The idea that one has to serve with the same people and develop relationships over years to have tremendous impact is simply not true. It may help to have continuity and long-term presence, but it is not required.

Through this story come some powerful questions. Lawrence

challenged his higher-ranking fellow officer. Though the Colonel Brighton of the film was not technically his superior, Lawrence was on some extremely shaky ground when he contradicted Brighton's declaratory statements.

This brings up the great question of how far one should go to develop a relationship with a counterpart. Does one point out the obvious falsehoods of fellow workers or senior personnel if by doing so one gains credibility with the counterpart? Where does one draw that line? How can one know where the line should be?

These questions present profound truths that need careful consideration. I would suggest that to do this safely in terms of career and relationships, one must understand the larger objectives and consequences of any disagreement.

In the case of Lawrence, he knew that Arab success was essential to British success. Therefore, risking so much to gain the trust of key Arab leaders was well within his mandate. That may not always be true in industry or governmental relations. Sometimes such statements cause losses of millions of dollars or risk coalition support.

Beware and be willing to be bold!

Lawrence is both a brilliant example of success in cross-cultural relations and a problematic example of working within one's own organization. The world and the military are different today. Additionally, he was not American, and thus he worked in a different organizational culture. I'm not sure he could get away with using the same methods in today's system. His actions were impressive in terms of cultural awareness and empathy, but he overstepped his bounds with respect to his own organization.

# Arab Strengths

*The same hospitality which was practiced by Abraham, and celebrated by Homer, is still renewed in the camps of the Arabs. The ferocious bedouins, the terror of the desert, embrace, without inquiry or hesitation, the stranger who dares to confide in their honor and to enter their tent. His treatment is kind and respectful: he shares the wealth or the poverty of his host; and, after a needful repose, he is dismissed on his way with thanks, with blessings, and perhaps with gifts.*

—Edward Gibbon[25]

In understanding a different culture, it is useful to recognize its strengths. The strengths typically identified in Arab culture are honor, courage, generosity, and hospitality. In this section, I will emphasize generosity, hospitality, and pragmatism. Understanding these three aspects of Arab culture is one of the most effective ways we can develop empathy that leads to influence.

## Generosity

A great many stories exist about the quality and depth of Arab generosity. In many cultural awareness training sessions,

---

[25] Taken from The Decline and Fall of the Roman Empire, Volume V, page 195. This book was written in 1788, and setting aside the comment about "ferocious," it is still remarkably true today.

a warning on generosity is included: do not praise an Arab's possessions too much or you will be offered the item. This is absolutely true.

In 2005, I was traveling in Yemen and stayed for a couple days in the port city of Aden. While there, I saw a model wooden boat in a museum and was interested to know if there was a store somewhere in the city where I could buy one. I was looking for a particular kind of boat similar to those used by the ancient Arab mariners. I linked up with a taxi driver and the two of us went to every souvenir shop he could think of. All they had were European-style sailing ships. Finally, my taxi driver took me to a furniture store where he had seen an Arab-style model boat in the past. The store did not have the boat, but they sent us to their adjacent furniture factory. One of the managers took us to the warehouse, but they did not have any, saying that they are rare. This manager called the general manager's office, and we went there. He had two boats in his office. Pointing at them, he asked which one I was looking for. I pointed to one, expecting him to indicate where I could acquire such a boat. He then called in his secretary and had her take the boat and clean it. I protested, saying that I did not want to take the boat from his office. He brushed aside my concern. When his secretary returned, he gave me the boat, and when I tried to pay him, he told me it was a gift from one friend to another. I refused several times—enough for any American to understand clearly that it was not my intent to take such an object from his office. It was to no avail. I traveled home carrying my new boat onto the airplane with me.

Throughout the Arab world, it is regular practice for rulers to forgive debts and prison sentences at times of religious celebration. It is common to read in local newspapers that a wealthy person has done some generous deed for a poor or suffering family. It is necessary for any leader to be seen by the populace as generous.

Generosity among Arabs is genuine. Generosity is also a way in which someone is measured. A person who is not generous risks being perceived as less cultured. You should be careful how you appear in your dealings with Arab associates. Are you too demanding of Arab generosity without reciprocating?

Generosity is not just specific to Arab culture; it is also encoded in Islam. *Zakat*, an annual donation to the poor, is enshrined in the Koran and considered one of the Five Pillars of Islam[26]. The expected donation is typically 2.5 percent of one's accumulated wealth, capital assets (including savings), and livestock and agricultural goods. Those who have money are expected to share their God-given blessings with those who do not enjoy the same. This is viewed as a sign of piety. One is not limited to the minimum, and those who have much typically give more. This giving is most common during the holy month of Ramadan.

It is important to understand that the generosity of a guest or host does not extend to business dealings. Do not expect generosity when bargaining over business deals. Understand where one begins and the other ends. I have witnessed too many US and Western officers miss the transition from generosity to business, and to some degree they were surprised. Normally such things are separated in time and space and are typically not mixed. It is important not to expect generosity to trump common sense or good business practice.

---

[26] The Koran presents the Five Pillars of Islam as the following: 1) the shahada (Islamic creed), which requires one to state the supremacy of God and the role of the prophet Mohammed as the messenger of God; 2) prayers (salah), which are to occur five times a day; 3) almsgiving (zakat); 4) fasting during Ramadan (sawm); 5) the pilgrimage to Mecca (hajj) at least once in a lifetime.

*Hospitality*
There is a very close relationship between generosity and hospitality. To a degree they overlap, but there is a difference worth noting. As I have said so many times already, nuances are critical!

While walking the streets of Aqaba, Jordan, with a fellow Jordanian officer, I told the officer that he did not need to escort me, as I knew that he had things that he needed to do and buy for his family. As he explained why he needed to stay with me, he said, "You are my guest, and the guest is a prisoner of the host." What a wonderful revelation! For those not used to the overwhelming hospitality of Arab hosts, as I was not, such treatment can seem overwhelming, and there were times that I did feel a little like a prisoner to my host.

There is a well-known folktale of a bedouin who offered a guest his prize racehorse for a meal because he had no other meat to provide. He would not think of not providing for one who had traveled to be with him. Maybe from another perspective this seems extreme. As folktales carry with them moral lessons, the lesson here is that no possession is worth not treating a guest with the utmost respect.

Sometimes I have seen Americans try to keep up with Arab hospitality. I advise against this. One should certainly be hospitable and welcoming as appropriate to one's own culture. Trying to outdo an Arab in this regard will only lead to overexertion on the non-Arab's part and the possibility of insulting the Arab as well. I have seen many cases where national pride turned hospitality into a competition.

Another place where some overstep is in taking advantage of the hospitality. Do not mistake hospitality for genuine friendship or even respect. Very few Arabs will ever treat a guest rudely. In fact, they typically treat every guest, regardless of personal feelings, with a similar level of welcoming. When a person assumes too much of the relationship early on, it is possible to do great damage. As in any culture, it is important to build relationships over time and through competence and trust.

## *Pragmatism*

I view pragmatism as one of the defining characteristics of Arabs. I do not think they would describe themselves with that term, but I think that it ranks with honor, hospitality, bravery, and piety as defining ways of thinking and acting.

By pragmatism I mean, essentially, that if it works, they do it. I think the root of this lies in Arab bedouin culture and Islam, as with so many other aspects of this culture. Any nomadic tribal culture must be pragmatic to survive. This is even truer of those cultures that live in harsh climates. In the desert, if something makes you more capable of survival or more able to enjoy a better life, then it is immediately grasped and applied. If it is unclear how a certain behavior or idea can provide an advantage, then the behavior or idea is abandoned or adopted at a much slower rate.

If one travels to museums throughout the Arab world, one tends to see depictions of early Islam and discussions on the spread of Islam. A common statement in these museum displays is that Islam was adopted because of its simplicity. There is a lot of truth to this, especially when one compares seventh-century Islam with seventh-century Christianity or Judaism, religions that were full of relatively complex ideas of the nature of God and the right way to worship Him. Christianity and Judaism are typically viewed as religions of orthodoxy, or the "correct way" to believe. They tend to view worship in terms of rituals, behaviors, and conceptualizations. I would categorize Islam as a religion of orthopraxy, or "correct action" in belief. It is a religion of doing and a religion of action. The Five Pillars of Islam include one about belief (acknowledge one God) and four about action (prayer, alms, Hajj, fasting). Most Muslims speak of what they must do to be pious. It is not uncommon in the Middle East to see men who press their heads against the ground in prayer so hard that they leave a nearly permanent bruise on their foreheads. This is one way in which they demonstrate their piety.

Another example of Arab pragmatism is their business model. Arabs have not historically been entrepreneurs. An entrepreneur is one who accepts risk to promote a new and innovative product or idea—entrepreneurialism involves going into the unknown. This behavior violates the "first thing" principle of CSM Washington in northern Alaska—survive. The Arab business model is the tried and well-tested model of the trader. The trader follows well-known routes with guaranteed products. He tends to travel in ways and in organizations that provide safety and as much as possible ensure survival. In modern terms this means new businesses do not get started in the Arab world until they are proven elsewhere, and then many will open in close proximity to each other despite the possibility of flooding the market. (This gets at a problem with planning and analysis and is different from the pragmatism issue.)

*handwritten margin note: + I hate oFT thought about this*

### *What does this mean in practical terms?*

Concepts are not well received and not usually clearly understood. This is not because of a lack of intelligence, but because of the educational methods of the Arab world. As previously mentioned, education—both religious and secular—is acquired through rote memorization. This means that creative and conceptual thinking is not highly valued or instructed. Seeing and doing are what make a difference. A few examples follow.

- If the US wants an Arab military to adopt a new doctrine, the American must show them this new doctrine. The Arab must watch it in action and see—or better yet, experience—the benefits of this new doctrine. "Maneuver" or "combined arms" are words that can mean many things. The Arab must see what the American means by those terms and feel that it is better. A senior Iraqi leader in 2011 suggested having Iraqi political and military leaders ride in a Russian-made T-72 tank and then in a US-made M1A1 tank. This is a great example of this type of experiential communication.

- Maintenance is a consistent challenge, as the idea of preventative maintenance is a philosophy not unlike religion. Since one cannot prove a negative, it is impossible to prove that a lack of preventative maintenance actually results in catastrophic failure. US officers trust the statistical data and studies, but these are not universally well received in the Arab world. I would suggest taking people to maintenance facilities or taking them to field training sites to observe maintenance in the field and to see the damaged and inoperative vehicles. US and Arab mechanics could then diagnose what went wrong, and those cases could be used as examples for how preventative maintenance may have averted the damage or the need for repair. The Arab mechanics, having experienced the problems firsthand, could now serve as spokesmen for the concept of preventative maintenance, and their opinion will likely be valued more highly among other Arabs than the opinions of the guys trying to make a sale.

- There are similar issues with repair parts flow. From a pragmatic view, parts in a warehouse represent power and control. Parts moving through the system represent a loss of control and therefore a loss of *wasta*.[27] Therefore, one needs to tie *wasta* to

---

[27] *Wasta* is an Arabic word that is best translated as "influence." It is best represented by the spider I earlier described, the one that is able to sit in the middle of the web and direct the actions and responses of other spiders. That is a spider that has *wasta*.

the parts flow and customer delivery and service rather than to the supply. This would mean showing an Arab counterpart and senior leaders a unit repairing vehicles after receiving repair parts, and then show them a full warehouse that does not get parts out. This might demonstrate the pragmatic benefit of parts flow and cause the senior leader to view with a critical eye those warehouses that are always full.

- If one wants to demonstrate the strength of training over equipment, then one could put US soldiers in T-72 tanks and have them demonstrate what well-trained crews can do in any equipment.

The simple answer to how to utilize Arab pragmatism is that one needs to demonstrate or show the counterpart the concept in practice rather than tell them. This requires additional time. It is one of the reasons things happen more slowly in this part of the world. (There are many other reasons as well.) An Arab counterpart will need to see, understand, contemplate, and come to agree before taking action. Once the counterpart does, in fact, agree, then things can move relatively quickly.

*How does this pragmatism affect how Arabs make military equipment purchase decisions?*

I am fairly certain that this line of thinking affects decisions in many Arab countries. These countries benefit from balancing and maintaining connections with multiple power players. In terms of military equipment purchases, the Middle East tends to maintain some balance between Britain, France, Russia, and China, at a minimum. All of these are UN Security Council countries. The reason is relatively obvious. This is strategic or strategic-benefit-oriented pragmatism. The interoperability of systems or the complexity of maintenance is irrelevant compared to the high-level benefit. They want to diversify. Too much reliance on a single country—even the US, with its superior equipment—is not pragmatic. Another point related to this is that interoperability is a concept rather than a reality to most of the decision makers. They probably do not understand what the US means by the term or how having a BTR-4[28] might be more problematic than having an M1A1. If one wants to emphasize inoperability, it is important to demonstrate and show the thinking and issues behind the term rather than only say it.

This pragmatism can be illustrated through an example purchase of Russian-made BTR-4 over US-made M113. The BTR-4 offers more capabilities the M113. It is an infantry fighting vehicle with cannon, machine guns, missile launchers, and smoke grenade launchers. Because this vehicle represents more capability, it is therefore of more benefit to the owner, and it is pragmatic to have such a vehicle. US equipment is expensive. A pragmatic person will prefer four of something for the same price to one of something else unless the one is manifestly better than the four combined. A US officer may be better off communicating how to use the new capability of the foreign system in concert with the US equipment rather than emphasizing only the US equipment and technology. Most Arab countries will have equipment from many nations, and they will need to integrate this equipment into a common framework of doctrine, tactics, techniques, procedures, and execution. US personnel need to demonstrate pragmatic thinking unless they want their ideas to be deemed irrelevant to the realities on the ground.

If kickbacks and graft do exist in some weapon sales in the region, then the pragmatism is obvious: one receives a personal benefit through a specific sale. Of course, the sale that results in the greatest personal benefit would be the sale pursued. Altruistic bureaucratic service is not usually pragmatic.

Most of what the US is trying to do in the region with respect

---

[28] Russian-made wheeled infantry fighting vehicle.

to both business and security-related engagement is pragmatically sound. The recommendations here center on the idea that we need to present our case like someone who is teaching rather than preaching. If one presents having professional noncommissioned officers, conducting preventative maintenance, using maneuver doctrine or combined arms, having a free-moving parts flow, or any number of other major transformational initiatives as if they are inherently right and correct things to do (like a tenet or article of faith), then there will be challenges in communication. These must all be **demonstrated** to the pragmatic mind and **shown** to be right. Once that is understood and accepted, the communication will flow—the pragmatic listener will want it and want to know how to get it. Eight years of US operations in Iraq were not sufficient demonstration because the desired audience did not know what they were seeing. One cannot assume that because someone witnesses one's activities they recognize the subordinate and necessary foundational principles. These elements need to be made explicit in the conversation rather than implicit.

# Walls

Previously I identified several areas where bees and spiders are different. Now I want to discuss the aspect of *walls*. What I mean by *walls* is a barrier to communication.

These are not simply misunderstandings or different ways of looking at things. These are areas where the difference in perspective is so great that when one takes such a position one is viewed as something akin to an idiot or lunatic. By espousing such views one raises the risk of immediately losing credibility.

What I am talking about now is much more than the different boxes I previously mentioned. As one imagines the two opposing figures in their different boxes, one should envision a physical barrier that divides the two counterparts or opponents so completely that even if one grows one's box, it is not sufficient to overcome the barrier. One needs to recognize the barrier and then seek a way to get around it.

Walls typically exist because one assumes that *the* way one sees the world is the way to see the world. The effort to force one's counterpart or opponent to see things from one's own perspective will typically not succeed. This is a failure that I encourage all readers to avoid. When I say that walls exist because of one party, that is not entirely true. A collision with a wall typically occurs because one party refuses to recognize the wall's existence and then seeks to drag their counterpart through the wall that they themselves do not acknowledge exists.

How can such collisions be avoided? Remember the earlier methods of success: introspection, empathetic appreciation, and empathetic expectation. In this case, they mean the following:
- Introspection: Why do I believe this to be true?
- Empathetic Appreciation: Why do they believe the opposite to be true?
- Empathetic Expectation: How can I get around, through, or beyond the wall?

I will elaborate through several examples. I will not go into great detail with any one example. Rather I will introduce some of the more common walls Americans have run into or ignored. Not all Arab subcultures are the same. Not all Arabs are the same. Engineers, pilots, PhDs in the Arab world may not see some of these issues as walls. Some Arab countries have much greater access to higher-level education abroad, where many of their citizens are introduced to Western and even bee-like ways of thinking. I say this as a reminder that one must not paint too finely with any of the brushes presented here. This is why it is so important to not just understand the larger society, but also the experience and perspective of the individual.

The following list of walls is not comprehensive, but includes several areas where I have personally observed cultural collisions.

### Limitations
#### *Americans: Budget Constraints*
It is true that the US government has a budget and that the US military is constrained to operate within that budget. This is especially clear to all those who work inside the US government. It is also true that US industry is also constrained by budgetary considerations. These are facts that every employee and manager deals with on a regular basis.

# The Box and the Wall

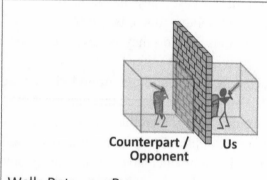

Counterpart /    Us
Opponent

Walls Between Boxes

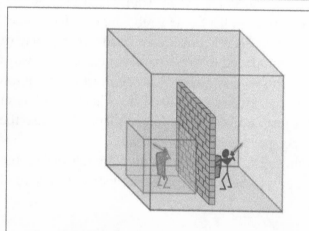

Walls Within Boxes

## *Arabs: US can do Anything*

Watch television or a recent movie from a foreigner's perspective. It is rather interesting what such programs reveal about the US. In such fictional portrayals, there are no constraints to US finances or the US military. We retask satellites at a command and track people through major metropolitan areas with tremendous speed and ease. The US also enjoys a reputation for being able to do anything. We won World War II, we built the first skyscrapers, and our streets are paved with gold (okay, that is a bit much, but it is interesting just how many believe something close to this). The point here is that people truly believe these things about the US. Just as the perception of most Americans about the Middle East is shaped through mass media of some sort, the reverse is also true.

The primary point here is that you cannot expect to be believed when discussing budgetary limitations. Your counterpart does not accept that these limitations exist. To an Arab, the American who goes on about such things is either being deceptive or is uninformed. Either way, he or she is not worth listening to. Even those who understand budgetary issues and are well informed will still not fully accept that US fiscal problems will result in hard reductions, as the difference in wealth between the US and the counterpart's country is so great. The poorer the counterpart's country, the deeper this opinion will be held—the thicker the wall, if you will.

## Importance of Training
### Americans: Training Is Dominant

Every US officer is taught that training is the key to success. It is interesting that in a society in which the individual is valued to such a great degree, the US military emphasizes the system of training rather than bringing out the particular skills of the individual. "Training is what creates success on the battlefield" could probably be considered a US military maxim. The US soldier believes that if he receives sufficient training, he can take a lesser quality piece of gear and be extremely effective on the battlefield.

Don't get me wrong—the US military culture loves technology and the best gear money can buy. That is absolutely true.

That said, if one makes a US soldier choose between an untrained squad with the most modern gear and a fully trained squad with older gear, I believe the US soldier would choose the older gear with the better training, because training is what wins engagements, battles, and war, or so we think.

### Arabs: Equipment Is Dominant

Listen to Arab commentators explain Israeli success or read Arab history or Arab editorials on the same topic. There is a recurring theme in all of them as to why Israel has been consistently successful against Arab opponents: technology.

Some Arab historians have implied and directly stated that the reason Anwar Sadat switched from the Soviet sphere of influence to the US sphere was because he realized that in order to achieve some technological parity with Israel, he needed US technology. True or not, this is a commonly held belief among many of the Egyptians with whom I have spoken on this topic.

Technology has been key to US success as well. The US media has certainly helped to create or emphasize this point, as so much of what it has shown regarding US military superiority deals with the *stuff* of conflict rather than the training. It was the stealth fighter and the smart bombs, the thermal imaging and heavily armored tanks that defeated Saddam Hussein during Desert Storm, not the pilot or the tank crew that operated the vehicle. As the media portrays, so the region believes.

If one were to ask an Arab soldier to select between an untrained squad with the latest gear and a fully trained squad with older gear, I believe this soldier would chose the latest gear over the training because it is the equipment that wins engagements, battles, and war, or so they think.

Because of how central training is to the psyche of US military leaders, this may be a difficult wall to avoid. Asking a US officer to avoid this point is like asking a Christian not to speak of Jesus or a Muslim to avoid discussion of Mohammed. That said, one needs to be aware of the wall so that one does not collide into it blindly. US engagers do not do enough to demonstrate this point. We typically show the end result of the training—the team breaching a door in a live-fire close-quarter engagement—but we typically do not lay out the resources (time, ammunition, targetry) expended to get this team to this point. As such it seems almost like magic that this trained team appeared once we had this great equipment. Rather than communicating the US bee perspective, we actually communicate and reinforce the Arab spider perspective.

## Training Cycle
### Americans: More Training Is Better

The US officer believes that training results in success and saves lives. The more training, the more success, and the more lives saved. General George S. Patton said, "An ounce of sweat in training saves a gallon of blood in combat," or words to that effect. This thought expresses the US perspective succinctly.

There is no level of training that is good enough. There can always be more. There are always more tasks to improve or more skills to develop. Within US training doctrine is a reference to training a primary individual and then training those who might need to perform that individual's tasks in the case of injury or incapacitation—the doctrine calls for a never-ending process of training.

All of this training comes with costs in time and material.

### Arabs: We Are Natural Warriors

Have you watched that scene in *Lawrence of Arabia* yet?

I hope so. If you have, then you heard the line from the actor Omar Sharif as his character banters with Colonel Brighton, who argues in favor of training. "Ha!" shouts Ali. "The English teach the bedouin how to fight?" This exchange is extremely telling and very critical in this discussion. Bedouin are natural warriors, and fighting is in their genetic code—or at least that is the line of thinking. Training beyond introducing the soldier to the gear is superfluous.

Following this line of thinking, training beyond operation and maintenance is not only unnecessary, but wasteful of critical resources. Fuel, ammunition, and repair parts cost money. Sometimes a lot of money. This part of the argument will sound like the one used for not conducting preventive maintenance. In many ways it is the same.

It is useful for US personnel to understand how costly their methodology is. Most countries cannot afford the insurance that this constant training provides. Like insurance, the goal is to never have to use it. Reflect on the billions of dollars in training that the US military spent throughout the 1990s. The US military only cashed in on a small portion of the investment, as most of the soldiers so trained left the military without ever firing a shot in anger. Was that money wasted? The answer to this question differs depending on perspective. When engaging on this topic, it is useful to think about the other side and understand the reasoning behind its thinking.

## Preventative Maintenance
### Americans: Prevent Problems

Preventative maintenance and wealth seem to go hand in hand. Those who believe in this practice accept the dictum that an ounce of prevention is worth a pound of cure.[29]

---

[29] Attributed to Benjamin Franklin.

### *Arabs: Avoid Unnecessary Costs*

If something is not broke, don't fix it. New equipment needs little to no maintenance. These two thoughts dominate the thinking of many Arabs and other cultures regarding this topic.

I have previously covered this topic in some depth, so I will only touch on it now. It is important to realize that this issue is a very significant wall. In my experience, the US side tends to explain the need for preventative maintenance as if they are talking to the already converted—we already agree, and therefore the process is as follows. As a result, the counterpart looks at the presenter as either crazy or stupid. Effective communication ends because unwittingly the American has run into a wall. Regarding this topic, points of view need to be shown and not simply preached.

As an example, when I worked with the foreign military sales of the M1A1 tank, I listened to requests for access to the maintenance history of the system and failure rates of parts. No such information was ever delivered. The pragmatic counterparts were requesting US personnel to demonstrate the average need for repair parts. Instead of providing the data and showing the argument, the Americans continued to use words to emphasize the importance of this principle of faith—some money spent now saves you much more money later. I call it a principle of faith because one cannot truly prove this to a skeptic's satisfaction, as this requires proving a negative—for example, the engine did not break because we changed the oil every 3,000 miles.

### Information Sharing

### *Americans: Share More Soonest*

The bee shares information so that the hive can act on the information and reap the collective benefit of the information. Information empowers individuals to make decisions that benefit both the individual and the group.

### *Arabs: Retain Information for Power*

The first thing is to survive, and survival requires that the individual has information that the group does not have. If everyone knows the same thing, all are equal and individual power dissipates, making it more difficult to survive.

This is another topic previously discussed, so I will only address it here in relation to the wall. The fact that sharing information can be seen as directly threatening survival makes it one of the most difficult walls to scale or break down.

One of the biggest challenges with this wall is that Americans do not often realize how much the two cultures are alike in this regard. Americans hoard and conceal information as well and for much the same reason. For example, most corporations maintain proprietary information for competitive advantage. Many intelligence organizations do not share all they know, as there is concern about protecting sources for specific organizational advantage.

We think that we don't do this, and because we are blind to the reasons for our own behavior, we collide with the wall. The best way through or around this wall is to understand why one hoards information and then approach the communication as if trying to convince oneself to share the information. This is why introspection is the first step to cross-cultural influence.

## Success

### *Americans: Success=Progress*

In the US, progress equals success. I began writing this book during a US presidential election, and one of the primary topics of the debate was a simple tagline: are you better today than you were four years ago? This rather standard campaign challenge holds within it the basic assumption that things must get better from one election cycle to the next, and if it doesn't, this is grounds to declare the incumbent a failure.

### Arabs: Success=Position

The movement that began in December 2010 in Tunisia and spread to several additional countries in the Middle East and North Africa was labeled the Arab Spring based on the apparent success of the will of the people in the spring of 2011. Many US pundits argued that this was a move for freedom and democracy. I will not attack this view. But when it came to the demands of the protestors, rarely was there any mention of enfranchisement or additional rights. The one demand that was universal was to throw the ruler out. In the Arab world, success equals position.

The point that is important here is how one engages on this topic. Typically, Americans use progress as a motivator when engaging with an Arab counterpart. As stated earlier, Arabs love progress as much as any other culture; however, one should not think that they see progress as synonymous with success. In the Arab view, progress reflects the ability of the leader to be "a river to his people." The leader's ability to retain his position defines his authority and power.

## Rules

### Americans: Consistency

Americans come from different worlds, different cultures. In many cases, those who arrive on the shores of America come from an oppressive environment where they may have been part of a subjugated minority or an abused group. The laws of the US are designed so that all—those from the wealthiest of families to those from the poorest caste—receive roughly equal treatment. To maintain this image, rules must be fixed. If everyone waits in line, then everyone has the same opportunity for service—how they are treated is not based on who they know or what ethnicity or tribe they are from. Rigidity, in this case, allows for a sense of equality, and for Americans equality is critical.

### *Arabs: Flexibility*

Rules are ideas. They give guidance. The Arab system is not about parsing the smallest task until a wrong is found and the perpetrator can then be punished. Following the rules is good, but the rules themselves have no sanctity or inherent value.

I was sitting with a group of Arab officers who shared with me some of their experiences in the US during military training. A story told by a young officer of a traffic citation best illuminates this wall. The young officer parallel parked his car, but crossed the parking space line by several feet. When he returned to his car from an errand, he found an officer writing a ticket. He spoke with the officer about why he was getting a ticket. The officer pointed to the line. The Arab asked incredulously, "I am getting a ticket for being three feet over a line?" Even in the office as I spoke with him, he could not believe the American insistence on rules to the exclusion of considering the person. Here was a human who needed to get something from the store and made a brief stop close to a parking space and returned quickly. From the Arab perspective, the US officer enforced a cold and unfeeling rule instead of thinking independently.

I once worked with two US police officers, and they regularly said how difficult it is to enforce rules unless they are enforced for "the lowest common denominator." The uniformity of enforcement is what allows police to remain free from suspicion and criticism of favoritism or breach of ethics.

These competing perspectives must be understood before explaining why the US government demands forfeiture of funds because the country was late in submitting a name by a week. How can hundreds of thousands of dollars be lost over a few days? What kind of partner enforces such rules? From one perspective, it is necessary to treat everyone the same, but from the other perspective, such an action is evidence of a lack of friendship, generosity, and hospitality.

The concepts discussed here do not cover all the walls into which we may collide when crossing cultures. They just elaborate on some areas in which I have personally observed the impact. These walls are present. Ignoring their presence will only ensure that collisions occur.

Just as with cars, collisions cause great violence to both parties, and they prevent necessary trust from developing. As I will show in greater depth in the final part of the book, it is important that your counterpart perceives you as one who "gets it" in order for you to be able to have influence.

Walls are those topics that will get you the "village idiot"[30] look if you address them in the standard American manner. Be wary of any of these topics during early parts of your relationship. If they must be addressed—and typically, they must—then do so slowly and only after you know how your counterpart perceives these same topics. Maybe your counterpart is an engineer by education and already believes in training and preventive maintenance. Then the topic is safe. This is about developing empathy prior to taking on the walls. Finally, do not talk through walls. Go to your counterpart's side of the issue and coax him or her to come along to your side.

---

[30] I am using phrases like "village idiot" and words like "stupid" and "crazy" to communicate the level of problems created by this behavior. There is no intent to belittle, insult, or poke fun at those for whom such labels have been medically or societally ascribed in the past.

# ⚘ Part Two Conclusion

Do your homework! Too often people enter meetings with cross-cultural counterparts and conduct them off the cuff. They have not done the work required to understand their counterpart in each way that understanding has value: religion, history, culture, language. Maybe I sound like a grumpy parent, but if your "grades" with respect to relationship building are not great, I would suggest that you have not properly done your homework. It is essential and foundational, and therefore it must be done first.

Demonstrate that you understand them. Show it. This is not a thing for discussion. It is important to greet them with the proper phrases, demonstrate the proper cultural behavior, share and discuss the proper stories, talk about and reference the proper historical anecdotes, and show deference and knowledge of the faith. This is all about walking the walk. If you are just talking the talk, then you will have poor "grades" in the relationship.

Do not be afraid to cross superiors if the situation demands it. Understand the situation thoroughly and know the boundaries that are crossable to stay employed. One does no good if one is unemployed. This comes from knowing the bigger interests of one's government or one's company over the smaller and sometimes petty interests of the current demand, request, or guidance. Again, I say beware and be bold!

See the walls and do not talk through them. Be cognizant of

the fact that there are truly cultural blocks to communication. See them and negotiate around them to the counterpart's side. Then invite the counterpart to come over to the other way of looking at things. The walls are real and are truly worthy of consideration. One can do a great deal of damage to future aspects of the relationship if one foolishly crashes into a wall or drags one's counterpart headlong into the wall.

# Part THREE

## Gaining Influence

# Gaining Influence

In some ways this book may come across as some Machiavellian dissertation on manipulating or deceiving an opponent.

Not at all!

In today's globalized world many in business and government are interacting across cultural boundaries. In such a world it is essential to understand the other world in order to be more effective in these endeavors. Sales and diplomacy are all about helping the customer or counterpart to see what the salesperson or diplomat sees. I am simply trying to make this process more effective by emphasizing cultural differences in human interaction.

The entire point of this book is to help people develop genuine influence in a cross-cultural environment. Everything preceding this leads to this point. Otherwise this book would simply be another version of the Culture 101 class. Take food with your right hand. Do not point the bottom of your feet at your counterpart, et cetera. Those classes fail by missing the "so what" that any student who stays awake in the class is thinking. The "so what" is gaining influence.

# Make a Connection

If one is trying to influence a spider, one needs to be connected to that spider's web. It really is that simple. This portion of the book explains some ways to make that connection. As stated in the initial warnings, this is not a cookbook. One cannot simply add a pinch of understanding and a cup of empathy and magically gain influence. I propose some suggestions and ways of connecting to the other and developing a relationship.

I want to emphasize that putting these suggestions into action with a cursory, utilitarian mind-set will ultimately lead to long-term failure. Making a connection and building a relationship with anything less than a sincere interest and commitment to do so will be seen as disingenuous and will erode and destroy the relationship. The final warning is to not let Arab generosity and hospitality cloud one's judgment or assessment of one's counterpart. No one comes out of a desert after hundreds of generations a fool.

### General Suggestions

As stated previously, do your homework and know something about your counterpart's religion, culture, history, and language. If done the right way, this can build nearly instant rapport.

Arabic is a language of poetry and social interaction. The first few minutes of nearly every meeting between two Arabic speakers is dominated by a barrage of phrases, questions, and answers that

154

all essentially ask "how are you?" These simple greeting phrases are relatively easy to learn and very useful in establishing an initial connection. Each country and even each tribe has some unique words or phrases in this give and take. Learn them. Using a local dialect for "how are you" communicates several things immediately: 1) that you appreciate Arabic language, 2) that you did enough homework to learn the local way of saying things, and 3) you understand the religious significance to the greeting. All of these things are good and immediately move you out of the "ignorant foreigner" category.

Be conversant in what is happening in their greater culture. Is there a holiday that they recently celebrated or are planning to celebrate soon? In most Muslim countries the weekend includes Friday. Though Islam does not have a Sabbath equivalent on which work is forbidden, Friday is the one day that most people do have off, as many work six-day weeks. Are they fasting? Obviously the entire Muslim world fasts during Ramadan, but there are other days as well when devout Muslims fast, and knowing this and showing sensitivity toward those who are fasting sets one closer to being "like us." Be aware of the culture and how that culture affects the lives of those within it, and then find small ways to demonstrate your understanding.

Know your *kunya.* This is the name that a father or mother takes when they have a son (or sometimes a daughter). In English we see it as *Abu* or *Um,* which means *father of* or *mother of.* What is the name of your oldest child? Is it a Biblical name? All Biblical names have Arabic translations, as the Bible has been translated into Arabic and many of the names are also found in the Koran.

I previously gave examples of both myself and another officer I knew in Iraq using our *kunyas* to great effect in making simple connections right at the beginning of a relationship.

Relationships are at the heart of spider behavior. They are

probably the key to making an initial connection.

When I was in Iraq, I heard many Iraqi leaders run through a mental rolodex of names when they met a new senior US leader. They would list all the senior people who had been through their command in an attempt to make a connection with this unknown American general. Once the US officer said that he knew one of the other names, the Iraqi would smile and express what a great relationship he had with that person. He would then continue with more names to strengthen the connection with his new guest through their mutual friends.

This method is useful and should be followed as well. Most military organizations and businesses outside the US are relatively small, and the senior officers in those businesses and militaries all know each other. Therefore an Arab businessman or officer assumes that if he knows a US officer who is an infantry officer and you are also an infantry officer, then you must be familiar with the other officer. It is very difficult for them to understand the sheer size of the US military or major US corporations, and therefore you cannot expect them to get the fact that you do not have personal knowledge of all other officers in your own company or military specialty.

If you do have a mutual acquaintance, you should use it to make that initial connection. Relationships can be and typically are one's bona fides in the Arab world.

### Personal Suggestions

What do you know about your counterpart? Is he or she married? How many children does he or she have? What ages are his or her children? Where did he or she go to college? What did he or she study? What village is he or she from?

In this laundry list of questions, one should get the idea that the more one knows about one's counterpart, the easier it may be to make a personal connection. A large part of this information is gained through personal interaction and conversation.

During my time in Iraq, I worked for a US leader who carried around pictures of his children, one of whom was to be married that year. Two of his sons and one of his daughters are army officers, and he regularly used the pictures of his children to begin conversations. A successful general officer whose children are following in their father's footsteps is an outstanding way to generate discussion about the counterpart's family, especially when one is among those who value a warrior ethos.

On one of my visits with an Iraqi counterpart, we got into a conversation about his background. He had been a fighter pilot in the Iraqi Air Force during the Iran–Iraq War, and had flown the MiG-15 and MiG-21. Over the course of our conversation it became clear that he missed flying. I did a brief search on the internet and found a model MiG-21 with an Iraqi decal. I did not regularly visit the official, so I relayed the information to those who worked with him more often. A great way to have made a connection would have been to purchase the model aircraft and give it as a gift. What a way to communicate that you listened and are interested in your counterpart.

**Be present!** It is difficult to overemphasize this simple statement. In the US, it is odd for a person to simply drop by to say hello in a professional setting. The expectation is that one needs to have some business worthy of the interaction. This is definitely not true in the Middle East. One needs to be making contact on a regular basis to communicate the importance of the relationship. This is especially true of mid- and low-level personnel. Some high-level people may be too busy to have such impromptu meetings. That said, such people will still usually take a call. I cannot count the number of times senior leaders received calls from people who were simply reconnecting.

The consistent meetings, phone calls, and visits communicate one's willingness to keep coming back. Just as people in the Arab world need to ask multiple times or refuse multiple times to be seen as sincere, they need to stay in contact to be viewed as serious about the relationship. A person who makes contact once a month or less is viewed as much less serious compared with a person who is calling or seeing the counterpart weekly. It is just that simple.

Making a connection is all about quantity time, not quality time. To really understand this, one needs to adopt the Chinese maxim that quantity has a quality all its own. Being present a lot allows for being present when one's counterpart is ready to discuss the topic at hand. I want to emphasize this point. **You need to be present when the counterpart is ready to listen, not just when you are ready to talk.**

Again and again I have seen a US military or government leader breeze into a room, conduct pleasantries, go through the laundry list of requests and issues, conclude with coffee, and then head out again. Typically the leader perceives the meeting as a success because all the right things were done and all the right things were said. Were the meetings successful? Not usually. Why, if all the right things were done and said? The answer is simple. The things were right; the timing was wrong.

An ethnic Palestinian who happens to be a US Army officer once said that nothing of value occurs in the Middle East before midnight. This means that most of the real business of negotiation and idea sharing happens much later in the day, during informal meetings held in the homes of senior people. During the drinking of tea and coffee, ideas are expressed between periods of silence and contemplation.

I told many US officers in Iraq that the best time to be an advisor was at these meetings wearing civilian clothes while drinking coffee and even watching television. One night, after many nights of sitting in these meetings and accomplishing nothing (from a bee's perspective), the Arab commander may lean over and say, "Tell me about this maintenance program of which you have been speaking." Then at the next staff meeting, the commander will lay out his plan for a new maintenance program. It would be his idea and he would be the sponsor now. Success. The relationship was built by consistent and timely presence. Monumental decisions are not usually discussed at 1000 hours (10:00 a.m.). They are discussed at 2200 hours (10:00 p.m.) or later.

One needs to be there for those precious moments when the mind is curious and open. Think about my previous comments on the scene from Lawrence of Arabia. That course-shifting meeting probably happened after midnight, after the key players had been sitting together for hours. Yes, this is a movie and probably a fictional event. The points derived from it are true all the same.

## *Translators*

This may seem like an odd place to talk about translators. The reality is that a translator is a tool that assists one in making a connection, especially if one cannot speak the language of one's counterpart. Here I will focus on some key issues that arise in translated environments and can negatively affect one's ability to make the connection.

The first and maybe most important rule is to coordinate roles and responsibilities between you and your translator. Maybe it doesn't need to be said, but I will say it anyway: do this before the meeting! I have seen translators used in many countries, most significantly in Iraq, where there were many Western non-Arabic speakers. In too many meetings there had not seemed to be a discussion of what the translator would or would not do, and over the course of the meeting the translator became a more central figure. Know your translator. What is his or her level of English language comprehension and communication? What is his or her level of Arabic (or other language) education, comprehension, and communication? This knowledge should drive your choice of vocabulary and speed of speaking.

It may sound cruel or cold, but it is true. A translator is a tool. He or she exists to facilitate your relationship with your counterpart. Nothing more. This is especially true with respect to the meeting itself. Outside the meeting a person may have a great relationship with the translator; the translator may be an advisor and serve many other roles. In the meeting, they must be almost invisible to the actual relationship building.

One of my theories for why translators had an ever expanding role in Iraq is that US personnel were so overwhelmed by cultural and linguistic differences that they just abdicated their responsibility for doing their homework to their translators. By doing that, their lives became much easier.

Do not let your translator be the one with the relationship! If this occurs, then you simply become the grocer, and as such you cannot even have a voice like a provider. The translator in this case becomes the provider bringing by the American delivery person. Bad!

One meeting serves as a perfect example of all the bad behaviors and critical issues regarding translators. We walked into an office to discuss the need for an additional purchase of lubricants for tanks. The Iraqi general greeted the US personnel with professional yet seemingly cold handshakes and then hugged and warmly greeted the translator. During the course of the meeting the Americans talked to the translator, and then the translator talked to the Iraqi general. The Iraqi general responded to the translator, and then the translator responded to the Americans. Rarely was there eye contact between the Americans and the Iraqi. When the translator used Arabic for an extended period to explain the complexity of a particular point, the Americans often digressed into side conversations in English.

It is essential that one speak directly to one's counterpart. The translator, as I have said, is a tool, never the focus of the discussion. He or she should translate everything you or your counterpart says in the first person as if they are simply a mouthpiece—which they are. I recommend not even looking at the translator when speaking. Eye contact should be kept with the counterpart.

There should only be one conversation going at a time: your conversation with your primary counterpart.

In final, simplify your language! Think about this for a moment. Let's assume that I speak English at a college level, and I am speaking with an Arab who speaks Arabic at a college level. For a translator to capture the nuances and meanings of everything that we are saying, that translator would need to speak both languages at the same level. There are such translators, to be sure. They are very expensive and typically only work with senior political and business leaders. If you are a minor figure in your company, I am pretty sure that such a translator will not be available. Thus it is important to realize that someone—you or your translator—will simplify the language. My recommendation here is that you ensure that it is not the translator who selects the simpler word, but you. I know what I want to say and am the most qualified person to judge the best word replacement as I go from college-level to eighth-grade-level (or lower) English vocabulary.

### *Hospitality*
Recognize that hospitality is important in making a

connection. Just as the difference between a provider and a grocer is nuanced, so is the manner in which one accepts or declines hospitality.

When I was notified that I would become a Middle East specialist for the US Army, I was an instructor at the US Army Armor School. At this school were many international officers from Arab countries. Once they knew I would be going to the Middle East, they wanted to share with me the particulars of their culture. In this setting I was first introduced to the concept that I could never refuse an offer of coffee or tea. I was very concerned then, as for religious reasons I do not drink coffee or tea. How should I deal with such a situation?

In these initial experiences and during my Arabic language training, I asked a variety of people the right way to deal with this dilemma. In most cases I was given a sort of standard Arabic line: *this is difficult.*

What I have learned over the years of dealing with this issue is that it is acceptable to refuse an offer, but never to refuse the hospitality. It is okay to decline a specific drink, even coffee and tea, if I provide alternatives. I drink herbal teas or juice or soda.

As an aside, asking for water is not the right move here. In the US, water is what one typically asks for to avoid being a burden to a host. In the Middle East, no decent host would willingly serve water to a guest—it is like an American serving dirt. It just isn't what is done. It is much better to ask for coffee or tea or another hot beverage than to ask for water. This is especially true if you are a guest in a counterpart's home. At the office there may be water available, especially if the counterpart is used to working with Americans.

The offer of food and drink is mandatory of a host, and the guest, as stated earlier, is the prisoner of the host and therefore should accept the hospitality. It is okay to decline additional offers, especially of chocolates or candies.

Gifts are a part of the hospitality. An invited guest will usually be offered a gift, and a good guest will typically provide one. If you have developed a connection with your counterpart and you are traveling abroad, it is good to think about bringing a gift back. Arabs regularly buy gifts for family and friends when they travel abroad. Buying a gift for your counterpart or the counterpart's children is a good way to demonstrate that you get it and also that you are a partner.

Sometimes working with Arabs can be frustrating, as they seem to have adult ADD; they are easily interrupted by phone calls, visitors, et cetera One of the reasons for this is that the counterpart does not want to be rude to those who are calling or visiting. He or she is trying to maintain or strengthen connections with them as well. This is not meant to be rude to the guest in the room; rather it is an attempt to continue to build the web. One needs to be aware of this while conducting meetings and avoid being put off by continued disruptions. Be ready to restate or recover the material already shared and then forgotten during the interruption.

I hope the previous paragraph causes you to question why meetings are so often interrupted during the workday. Depending on the Arab country or culture in which you find yourself, the workday is probably not when things truly get done. This is not when the real meetings take place. Remember the earlier discussion about being present when your counterparts are ready to listen? Ten o'clock in the morning is probably when they typically greet those who pass through the office. It is when they sign memoranda and accomplish the mundane tasks of the day. Profound and important topics may not be discussed and shared then. Those may be reserved for meetings in the *majlis* or *diwan*[31]

---

[31] *Majlis* and *diwan* are different words that mean essentially the same thing: a gathering of respected persons for discussion, socializing, and possibly consultation.

later in the evening. Rather than them being interrupted by these seemingly unexpected visitors, it is probably the meeting that you arranged at ten a.m. that is the true interruption in their day.

# Create a Mediator

ediation is the nature of engagement in the Middle East. Most American youth grow up being told that they need to confront bullies, harassers, et cetera. The attitude in the West is that direct confrontation and direct communication is best and simplest for achieving results.

Imagine a car accident. There is direct interaction. There is confrontation. How is the situation resolved? It is not resolved by the arguments or physical altercation. It is resolved as the individuals involved exchange insurance information and police arrive to adjudicate fault and write a report that is, in turn, provided to the insurance companies to assign appropriate financial responsibility. In short, this emotional human interaction is dealt with through the mediation of the police and insurance companies. The problem is not resolved through direct confrontation.

I have watched the aftermath of traffic incidents in the Arab world on several occasions. There is usually tremendous emotion and, at times, violence.

This was discussed at sufficient length in the first part of the book. I bring it up here to express the importance of the principle. One needs to understand, accept, and appreciate the role of the mediator in the culture.

Then a mediator should be utilized in any engagement plan. This is especially true if a person is having difficulty in getting a critical point across. There is real benefit in reaching out to a mutually respected third party who may be more inclined to accept the new concept and who will then act as a mediator and advocate with the target audience.

This will be discussed in greater detail in the following section. The importance here is to let go of the single-track idea that engagement is all about direct communication.

# Build a Web

To function in a world of spiders, one needs to build a web of one's own. In my observations of engagements between bees and spiders, it is clear that bees think about direct action and direct engagement, as was previously stated.

Rather than mediation or building the web of connections, a bee looks at trying to influence the individual. In some cases the bee searches for the key decision maker and then invests all effort in shaping the thinking of that key individual. Influence is about shaping the thinking of a counterpart—moving them in their thought process, if you will. Much of this section will discuss this idea of movement as the goal of influence. It is important to understand that this is not real physical movement. It is conceptual movement.

The first lesson is recognizing those who influence the counterpart in question. To whom does he or she turn to understand issues and shape his or her decisions? Those people may be inside or outside the organization. They may be superiors, subordinates, peers, or rivals.

As one builds this web of connections, it is essential to remember the importance of being a provider personally and professionally. This may run counter to company or organizational rules and regulations. I recommend that you figure out a way to adjust or change the rules or get exceptions to the policies so that you can perform in the necessary role. If necessary, consider using personal funds to provide gifts.

Think in the terms of your counterpart. How does he perceive the influencers? Maintain consistent contact to demonstrate the seriousness of the initiative you are trying to move forward. To accomplish this you will need to visit regularly whether there is real business to discuss or not. Be there. It is okay to simply stop by to say hello. There will be an expectation of progress, and the better one can keep the counterpart informed of what is happening, the more you will seem like a provider even if you are only providing information. If nothing else, just make contact with your counterpart by phone to let him understand that he is important in making this key event happen.

### Example Web

While viewing this series of diagrams, it is important to keep in mind that this is a discussion on conceptually moving the counterpart toward a new way of thinking.

As previously stated, bees tend to engage directly with the decision maker. In a military organization, for example, one typically goes to the commander. If that doesn't work, then the approach is hierarchical and still direct. Go to the commander's commander. In this example one has the primary engagement target. The engagement is seeking to move the counterpart in a particular conceptual direction. For the sake of this discussion there is a primary rival of the counterpart, one who may threaten the counterpart's *wasta*.

If the current engagement method doesn't work, then the usual next step is to begin additional engagements—engaging harder with more people or higher-ranking people. What this method misses is that people do not exist in a vacuum.

Rather, the counterpart lives in a veritable galaxy of other individuals, and most of these other individuals have some

# Moving a Target, Part One

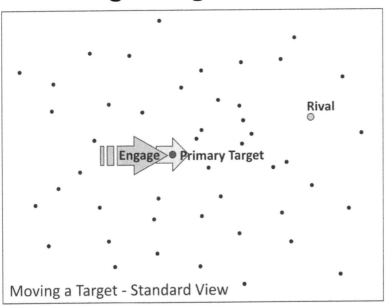

Moving a Target - Standard View

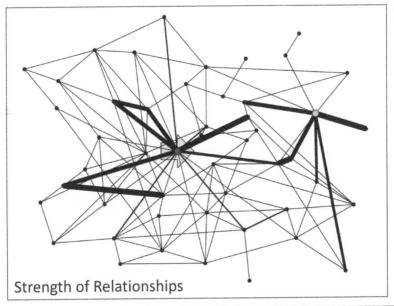

Strength of Relationships

# Moving a Target, Part Two

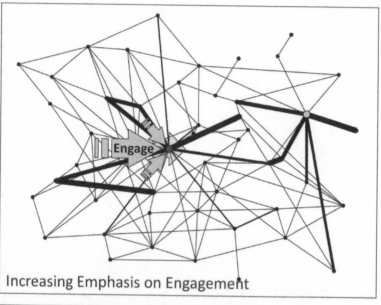

Increasing Emphasis on Engagement

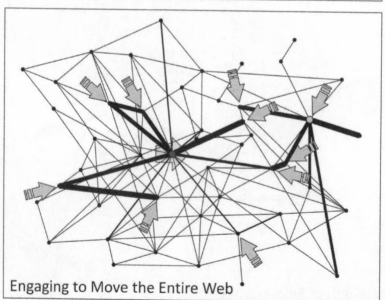

Engaging to Move the Entire Web

connection to the counterpart. In this example, each of these connections has a different degree of strength. Some of these connections are great friends with tremendous influence, and others are casual acquaintances with limited influence. It is important to keep in mind that, even though a rival may be the opposite of a friend, such an individual may still have a very powerful connection to the counterpart one wishes to influence.

So rather than following the standard pattern of directing one's engagement solely toward one's counterpart and engaging more deeply when additional movement is necessary, look at dispersing your engagement efforts so that they target not just the counterpart, but also those individuals who influence the counterpart.

This engagement dispersion may include engaging the counterpart's rival and those who influence the rival. This may force or inspire movement on the part of the counterpart.

If one's counterpart is reticent to move from the safe area of his web, it may be necessary to move the entire web. Thus the safe area of the web is now where one wants the counterpart to be, and the conceptual shift is no longer threatening to the counterpart's position.

This is not to be confused as an issue of progress versus position. The position needs to be safe for the progress to occur. The assumption here is that the desired conceptual movement is considered progress.

### Use the Connection

Once one has a connection, then one can use the connection. The connection is a lot like a bank account: one makes deposits by doing all the right things and being present. Once one starts using that connection, then one will be, in effect, making withdrawals. The challenge is to not overdraw the account. This typically occurs when one asks too early in the relationship for significant favors or assistance and goes into debt. Or, worse, when the withdrawal is refused as the request is obviously beyond the amount deposited. One needs to continually make deposits throughout the relationship. To do this right, one cannot simply build a relationship for the sole purpose of getting a single positive answer. Such behavior will be perceived by your counterpart and will fail much more badly than if you had not even attempted culturally informed influence.

The right way to use the connection is to follow the earlier example I gave. Be a provider! Do not put yourself in the position of the grocer. Recognize the nuanced differences between the two roles and learn to effectively play the position of the provider. The key nuance is the ability to provide that which you would have given anyway. This isn't about the what of providing, but the *how*.

Using a connection is not simply about doling out cashew-stuffed dates or new laptops. Once one makes a connection with an Arab counterpart, one can expect to be invited into an extended relationship network: weddings, visa requests, recommendation for college entrance, birth announcements, and all the other aspects of Arab social life. To do it right, one must be willing to go the entire way. The point here is the importance of understanding what all of that means.

# It's ALL about Them (Spiders)

have sat in numerous meetings in which the topic of discussion was why. Why did the counterpart not show for the meeting? Why was the counterpart so aggressive in questioning during the conference? Many other similar issues were associated with that interrogative most often linked to frustrated questions about cross-cultural issues.

In seeking to answer these questions, the common approach has been to look at the US as the cause of the actions or comments. Upon reflection, this is a rather arrogant method. Is everything about the US? Do relationships with US personnel, US representatives, or US companies serve as the cause for all decisions or actions in the Middle East? Absolutely not!

In a considerable majority of cases the opposite is true. It is all about them, the spiders. In our desire to understand the reasons and causes for decisions and actions, it would do us well to draw on everything we understand of the other culture to see why the counterpart's actions make sense within his or her context. The better we understand the other culture, the easier it will be for us to recognize the answers to the why questions from the perspective of the counterpart.

This general theme will be addressed here and in the following section.

Simply stated, what your counterpart does is more about his

or her web and network than it is about your request or presence. What about them is moving them toward this action? Will their attendance or nonattendance at a particular event have a positive or negative effect on their web connections? During the meeting, will their silence or participation enhance their standing in their web? Does their web require that they attack the presenter or support the assertions made?

All of these questions drill in at the heart of the individual's position and safety within his or her own web. I assert that every time a counterpart attends a meeting, he or she is there to affect the strength of the web and/or the size of the safety zone of the web.

# Recognize Your Role(s)

As a young cadet I was taught that when I stood at a podium as a presenter, I was there to be the subject matter expert and I needed to know my material. Not much later my instructors added that it was better to admit when I did not know something rather than to make something up; however, such instances needed to be rare. In such training my instructors tried to instill in me the importance of being fully prepared. That is all good.

When one stands before a group of Arab officers in a meeting or briefing, one needs to be prepared and proficient. One also needs to recognize that it is not sufficient to play a single role. This is not solely about being the subject matter expert. The presenter may need to also take on the persona of a mediator, advisor, whipping boy (or girl), or even a victim.

I have observed many meetings in which the Western presenter failed to grasp the need to take on a different role and instead clung desperately to being the expert; as such, the presenter missed an opportunity to grow the relationship.

I will briefly address some roles and what they mean in this context.

## Expert

In short, an expert is one who knows the answer and is precise. If one is playing this role, then one must understand the context of the answer in terms of background, prior decisions, and causes for changes and adjustments. It is also important that the expert have the facts clear and readily available. Arabs, in general, have great memories for facts and figures. This comes, in part, from an education system that hones this skill set. If you wing it when reciting facts, your counterparts will detect your ignorance.

## Mediator

I once observed a senior Arab officer ask a question on a topic about which only he or another more senior officer had the authority to make a decision. The presenter retained his role as expert and tried to answer the question, which in turn started a series of loud and contentious debates.

As I watched the interchange I reflected on the fact that the presenter should have taken on the role of a mediator. This would have allowed him to reflect the question back to the questioner. "Excellent question, sir. May I ask how you would organize your forces in this situation?" The question could also be redirected toward the most senior officer present, if that officer was the most appropriate decision maker for the topic addressed. Such a reflexive response would allow the senior leader to then pontificate and provide guidance. It would also free the presenter from having to force an answer that may not be the most easily accepted.

This is not a recipe. It is important to read the situation carefully and understand the players well enough to know the right time to slip into this role. That said, it is also important to remember that mediation is one of the most respected roles for a person to play in this region.

## Advisor

Just because one holds a title of advisor does not mean that one's counterpart wants to receive advice continually, regularly, or even seldomly. Advice in the Middle East comes from the wise and respected. Wearing a uniform that says US on it or carrying a business card that says "consultant" does not immediately grant the designation of wisdom and respect. Thus one needs to carefully weigh when it is most appropriate to offer the first element of advice.

What are the goals of the counterpart? What are the organizational goals? Do you understand the history and context of the current situation and who made the decisions that brought the organization to its current circumstances? These are dangerous waters, and just because an invitation to the pool was extended does not mean that it is acceptable to immediately jump in and splash around.

Deference and respect are two crucial watchwords when seeking to take on the role of advisor, even when the counterpart is seemingly open to and interested in advice. Offer it sparingly and cautiously. Advice is a dish that can easily overstuff the recipient.

### Whipping Boy

A whipping boy is one who takes punishment for another. There are times when this role is important and even essential. This is especially true for advisors and consultants, but may also apply to those in other positions. This role is closely linked with the final role of victim. In this case one needs to understand when to admit fault, whether actual or perceived, and take the beating (so to speak) for the counterpart. By doing so, the connection with the counterpart can sometimes be improved. Use this role judiciously and make sure the relationship can be enhanced by adopting it. If one were to adopt this role without the probability of improving a connection, then one is not actually a whipping boy, but simply an errant grocer.

### Victim

When adopting this role, the presenter becomes the evil American or Westerner who is to blame for all the ills inflicting the rest of the planet.

This is a role that I have seen used or avoided in unhealthy extremes. One can apologize, take the blame, and accept guilt too often. It is also possible to hold too strongly to the belief that one is always right or always on the high ground. No one is always right and no one is always wrong. As is true with any of the roles, do not assume it too readily.

That said, it can be useful to take the blame if by doing so one can advance the issue. If the debate is stalled on who is to blame, then take the blame, be the bad guy or girl, and then move the conversation forward so that the group can discuss really important and transformative issues.

When reflecting on these roles it is truly important to realize that the role is not determined by the presenter. The role should and must be determined by what the situation and the counterpart require. Flexibility is an essential element in this discussion. The following maxim applies:

> *Do not always try to be what you want to be. Be what the situation requires you to be.*

# Part Three Conclusion

Making a connection is basic relationship building. The cultural aspects of the cross-culture dynamic are the details, but the principles are essentially the same whether one is developing a relationship with one's in-laws, with extraterrestrial aliens, or with a culture from another part of Planet Earth.

American and Western notions of direct relationships and direct interaction are appropriate in some settings and with some individuals. This is true even among Arabs. It is also important to cast a broader net and make a web for oneself to build the influence one seeks. Develop relationships for the sake of the relationship, not solely for some possible monetary or organizational benefit. Sincerity will show and will be one of the best resources one has in seeking influence.

Know your roles and when it is appropriate to play each one.

In the effort to create influence, don't lose sight of the overall goal. This is a long-term process. Though T. E. Lawrence developed influence in a matter of weeks and months, very few of us are T. E. Lawrence. For the rest of us this is a matter of patience and consistent effort. It was for him as well; he just happened to be gifted at it.

Part of the greatest challenge for military members is their belief that they must achieve success in a deployment cycle. There must be influence, and progress must be demonstrable. Such an attitude risks true influence for the false influence of the grocer. So long as a grocer is delivering product, customers will come. Once the product ceases, customers cease to come and influence ends. In a world of diminishing fiscal resources I believe that the longer and less fiscally demanding course for influence is the better route.

# Final (Politically Incorrect) Thoughts

When I present this topic, I title the slide "Make No Mistake." I do this to point out that one should not make the mistake of failing to recognize the following points. These points are not popular, and few—if any—want to acknowledge them. Despite what people want to hear, these statements contain truth. These statements will appear bold, and as such there will be specific anecdotal evidence that contradicts them. But in my total experience, and in the experience of fellow specialists, natives, and others with whom I have discussed these issues, they hold true.

To get the full brunt of the truth, ride in a taxi with a local driver and ask him what he thinks about a given topic. Be ready to receive some uncomfortable advice and information. Like bartenders in American movies, Middle East taxi drivers see and hear much, and given an opportunity they will say much as well. I think the world would be better connected if senior leaders took taxis more often than armored sedans.

An earlier chapter discusses why Arabs don't like America. Make no mistake, they (fill in the blank with Iraqis, Jordanians, Syrians, et cetera) don't like us, and do not trust us. The latter part is especially important, because even the ones who do like us do not trust us. As previously stated, they have been humiliated by US actions and by the US and Western presence in their countries. Even US business presence can serve as a form of humiliation because the local economy cannot provide the same product or service.

I have regularly heard "you are as my brother" or "you are more than my brother." One such story helped me to put such flowery and comforting statements in context. I was sitting at lunch with an Arab battalion commander, his staff, and a visitor from their headquarters. Over the course of lunch I was told that the guest was "as my brother" by the commander. A few moments after lunch ended, I was asked by the same commander to deny the guest the use of a resource I had because the commander did not want the guest to look too good before the headquarters committee to which he was to report. "As my brother" was an Arabic exaggeration and needed to be taken as such. Make no mistake about the fact that you are a foreigner and will not, except in the most extreme of circumstances, ever become "as a brother."

Make no mistake, they are not "coming around." I heard so often in Iraq that the Iraqi army was coming around to a US way of thinking. No, they weren't. Too many Americans were selling themselves on their own success. Just because a spider is pollinating flowers does not make that spider a bee. It has been interesting to watch how each country in which I have served has more or less aggressively pushed back against US advice with the intent to do things their own way. They are spiders and want to remain spiders. Please do not kid yourself. Arabs, as pragmatic and intelligent people, will adopt US and Western techniques and behaviors when they realize that such will provide real benefit. Such specific action does not necessarily mean that they are coming around conceptually. Such a belief may cause those who work in this region to overreach and assume too much.

Make no mistake, we do not want them to become bees. I

have been in some miserable places on the Jordanian–Syrian border, along the Egyptian–Israeli border, in Iraqi brigade and school commands, and elsewhere where soldiers were living under hard conditions for years. The Arab militaries and companies we interact with are going to stay wherever they are, forever. They are not on a deployment. They do not serve for a limited duration before returning to Des Moines for a break from it all. They will be at the ready and in their home country until they die. If sleeping longer, drinking more tea, and doing fewer patrols allows that soldier to be happy and satisfied in his duty, then we should support such a style of behavior rather than trying to force them to change their military or business practices to the point that they would not be content in their own homes.

A spider who becomes too much like a bee will no longer be able to influence other spiders. I have watched over and over again as those who become "like us" lose more and more influence in their own military or community until they have no value for us. That sounds selfish, I know. It is also true that such bee-like spiders also run the risk of losing their position, as they may be perceived as being too American and therefore a security risk to their own country and people.

In the end, we want them to be satisfied in serving their country for a lifetime and not simply a year.

# The Conclusion

At the beginning of this book I asked a couple thought questions. I hope that you have reflected on them. As a reminder, here are the questions again.

1. Why are you here? *(Here* may be whatever cross-cultural environment you are in.) Are you here to accomplish tasks? Or are you here to create an environment of influence?
2. Is sitting in a person's office drinking coffee and tea for an hour and a half a waste of time?

Each reader may have developed different thoughts and responses. I will briefly describe my thoughts and answers.

The first question is individual. I believe that those who are most effective in the Middle East are those who are in the region to create an environment of influence. This is not to say that positive effects cannot be achieved by focusing on tasks. An active bee person can accomplish a great deal in the Middle East, especially if partnered with the right personalities in the region. The dynamic here is that such accomplishments will only last so long as the bee is present to push the activities. Once the bee leaves, the energy will depart.

Task accomplishment as a focus of behavior was demonstrated by the US military in Iraq for eight years. In this environment, the US achieved influence through the barrel of a gun. I am not saying that we threatened Iraqis with weapons. The reality is that we are the most powerful military in the world, and we were present in Iraq in force, advocating certain activities and policies. The fact that we were armed provided movement toward these activities and policies. The violence and political challenges in Iraq and the unwillingness of Iraqi leaders to coordinate with US leadership following the withdrawal of US forces shows the long-term failure of such attitudes. We had influence because we had the power of force. Once the power of force was removed, the influence was removed as well.

Throughout this book I have tried to differentiate between the immediate influence of activities and the real influence of relationships. I believe that relationships can build influence that lasts and can truly be transformative. It takes longer and can require a tremendous amount of patience. In the end, the gains will be worth the investment.

I have spoken to hundreds of military advisors and trainers. My advice is always the same, and I believe it is a hard and important truth. One who focuses on tasks may accomplish tasks, but that individual may not have a significant relationship or lasting influence. One who focuses on the relationship may build a significant relationship, and through that relationship be able to accomplish tasks.

A specific example is that of force protection and security. The US military had been in Afghanistan for more than ten years when in 2012 the so-called green-on-blue attacks became a serious problem. The quality of US force protection and security measures were never higher. No force in the world was better armored and better armed, yet our "friends" and "allies" were shooting and killing US soldiers as those soldiers were training and advising them. Why? All the physical protection in the world cannot protect an occupying military as well as a positive and effective relationship can. The best force protection one can have is the goodwill and active support of the populace. That is never derived through the near-imprisonment of US soldiers on camps comparable to maximum-security prisons. Engagement and developing influence not only leads to the accomplishment of tasks, but to a more secure working environment.

As question two is directly linked to question one, the answer should be clear. Drinking coffee and tea in a person's office for an hour and a half in the Middle East is not a waste of time. It can be a critical part of building the kind of relationships necessary for success. The challenge is convincing others of the value of such activities, as most bees do not see this as anything other than wasting time.

My last war story also comes from Iraq. During my first several months there, I regularly met with Iraqi government counterparts. Since I always needed a second person to be with me, I had to convince someone else to come along. This was not easy. One of my workmates seemed to really get it, and I thought he and I saw eye to eye. After several visits he said to me, "I can see that speaking the language makes a huge difference, as you have accomplished more in a couple days than others in the office have in a couple months. These meetings are not a waste of time." I was surprised that he was just getting it. I had been wrong about him earlier; he had simply been humoring me by coming along as an excuse to escape the office and get out of work. It was good that he began to see the value in the meetings. The critical point here is that one cannot assume that the message of influence building through engagement, understanding, empathy, and relationships is obvious or well understood. Relationships need to be built with the bees as well as the spiders to make sure they are willing to make the journey to develop influence.

I wish all who try the greatest of success! The world needs more real influence.

CPSIA information can be obtained
at www.ICGtesting.com
Printed in the USA
BVHW082333240419
546409BV00001B/76/P